741.6   ILL.

ILLUSTRATION WEST 33

A catalog of the 33rd consecutive annual exhibition by
The Society of Illustrators of Los Angeles
held in Murray Feldman Gallery at
Pacific Design Center
West Hollywood, California

August 13th through August 27th, 1994

PUBLISHED BY
Dimensional Illustrators, Inc.
362 Second Street Pike / Suite 112
Southampton, Pennsylvania 18966 USA
Telephone: 215.953.1415
Fax: 215.953.1697

PRODUCED BY
Society of Illustrators of Los Angeles
116 The Plaza Pasadena
Pasadena, CA 91101 USA
Telephone: 818.952.7452

DISTRIBUTED TO THE BOOK TRADE AND ART TRADE
IN THE U.S. AND CANADA BY
Dimensional Illustrators, Inc.
Southampton, PA 18966 USA
Telephone: 215.953.1415
Fax: 215.953.1697

DISTRIBUTED OUTSIDE THE U.S. BY
Rotovision SA
9 Route Suisse
CH-1295 Mies, Switzerland
Telephone: 41.22.755.3055
Fax: 41.22.755.4072

PRINTED IN SINGAPORE

Library of Congress-in-Publication Data
Illustration West 33
Society of Illustrators Los Angeles

ISBN #1-885660-00-6

TABLE OF CONTENTS

JOHN ROWE

My father used to take me to the library when I was a kid to check out books like *Tom Sawyer* and *Huckleberry Finn*. To this day, I can still clearly remember the paintings in those books, the ones that brought the story to life. Soon after, I discovered the writings of Robert Louis Stevenson, and every time I went to the library I'd go to the shelves to the books that had his name on them. I knew that I could always find a great story with great paintings about sailing ships and pirates and other really great stuff. I would look at the side of the book to see how many shiny pages there were, because I knew every one of them had a wonderful painting on it. I'd look at every painting and read the caption before I would check out the book. In these books I thought I had found a secret world that was mine alone. Years later I was to discover that these books, with painting by N.C. Wyeth, had enchanted many imaginations, along with mine.

Later on, it was the *Child's Encyclopedia of American History*. Each page had a full-color painting on half of the page, with copy on the other half. The American Revolution, the Westward Expansion, everything was illustrated – I read all twenty volumes! At the same time there was interest in the space program and the effort to reach the moon. Time-Life had a book with a cut-away of a Saturn 5 Rocket, every detail of the great rocket – the capsule, the engines, the heat shields, the controls, the landing module-all were precisely rendered. I spent hours dissecting that illustration, dreaming about space flight. From then on, I was captivated by the power of illustration.

For me, this is the meaning of illustration. Images that explain an element of life to an inquisitive child or adult. The illustrations in this publication do the same. None of us is N.C. Wyeth, nor should want to be, but each of us seeks to engage and inspire with the illustrations we create. The bread-and-butter projects of illustration: advertisements, magazine articles, products, books and spot drawings, all can become more than images created to secure an income or delight the art director or impress our peers. A few of them may become images that teach, foster political or social debate, evoke compassion and thoughtfulness, or make another child read and think about life a little bit more. Few professions offer this influence and timelessness, or such responsibility. By finding a new audience, the images in this book will continue to motivate in ways not yet realized. If we are really lucky, maybe the image that a child remembers will be one that comes from the best part of who we are.

Even now as I thumb through a book or magazine I think "that sounds interesting, maybe I'll read it, but first, let me sit down and look at these illustrations."

TERRI STARRETT

What a success! This beautiful annual is the Society of Illustrators of Los Angeles' "dream come true." It is the Society's wish to produce a book containing the awe-inspiring illustrations submitted each year in response to the Illustration West Call for Entries. All the categories were filled with excellent work. Elegance, expressive intimacy, and technical brilliance are an inherent quality of the illustrations submitted and placed like jewels upon the pages of this annual.

Illustrators challenge us to see things in new ways. They provoke thought, interpret ideas, inform and entertain. The arrangement of light, angle or perspective, and expression of mood capture the artist's personal expression. To be successful as an illustrator is a formidable undertaking. Thank you for allowing the Society to portray this amazing talent and creativity. To be included in this annual is truly an accomplishment. Congratulations to everyone in the Illustration West 33 annual!

THE EXHIBITION

In the spring of each year, after months of planning and preparation, the Illustration West Call for Entries is sent out across the nation. The call is answered, and the entries pour in. Once received by SILA, each entry is catalogued, assigned an identification number, then sorted by category. On the first of two consecutive days, one jury sees all of the Editorial, Book, Institutional and Student entries. Advertising, Entertainment, Medical, Self-Promotional/Unpublished, and Black & White categories are seen the next day by the second panel.

Actual judging day arrives bright and early. After everyone is settled with coffee, Pepsi and donuts, the work begins. Each judge is given a tabulating button that is wired to the judging machine in the back of the room. When a judge presses his or her button, a light on the tabulating machine flashes and the votes are recorded manually. Neither the judges nor the staff counting the votes knows which judge is voting for what. Each entry, when projected, is identified only by category and use. Illustration West is the only national juried illustration exhibition in which the judges do not have access to the names of the entrants while they are in the process of judging the show.

After a preliminary round and elimination in each category, the judges break for lunch while the staff condenses the slides down for the second round. The judges then narrow down the work to usually five or eight pieces in each category for medal consideration. The gold medal winners in the Advertising, Entertainment, Editorial, Book, Institutional, and Black & White categories are then considered for the Best Of Show Award and the Award for Excellence. Duplicate slides are made of the two top choices for these awards and sent to each of the ten judges to rank again in order of preference. In doing this, all the judges participate in choosing the two top honors in the exhibition.

On the day following the final judging, notification is sent to all who entered the competition. It is only seven weeks from entry deadline to the opening night reception, an amazing accomplishment for the judges, artists, volunteers and staff to achieve!

MONICA HEATH

"I have come to realize that artistic expression only exists as a serious and valuable possession insofar as one makes it his own. We have such a remarkable example in Homer. He knew light and shade, value, drawing, etc., in common with the others. Further than that, all he possessed was distinctly his."
-N.C. Wyeth on Winslow Homer

Every year when I open the entries, I am continually amazed by the new work, the new artists, the rich diversity in American illustration. It is heartening to see so many artists producing beautiful work that crisply reflects their personal character-that same distinctive artistic expression Wyeth admired in Homer.

On these pages are the distinct illustrative visions of 190 artists. Admire these images, they are the end result of much originality, sweat, thoughtfulness and joy. Learn from these images, too. What one has struggled with and triumphed over can inspire and ignite another. Examine these pages, and walk away from this book with something – there is an abundance of ideas to grasp. While doing so, remain true to your own singular vision. Desire to be an artist who speaks from your own emotions. Set values and goals that are high, and make all that you are distinctly you.

Thank you to the hundreds of illustrators I've met for teaching me new things about people and art. Many hours of enlightened conversation with thoughtful, discerning people is truly a gift you all have given to me. This exhibition and subsequent publication have been a joy to work on-thanks to such warm and intelligent friendships. I'm looking forward to making more with next year's production.

ACKNOWLEDGMENTS

Thanks to those who helped to make this exhibition and publication possible.

SILA members who contributed their time and energy: Charles Bloomer, Steve Chorney, Gary Eldridge, Lisa French, Diana Fritch, Nixon Galloway, Deanna Glad, Danilo Gonzalez, Jeffrey Hitch, Sylvia Hofflund, T. Pat Leary, Alvalyn Lundgren, Jeffrey Marx, Lorraine Maschler, Beth Massari, Gary Meyer, Serge Michaels, Briar Mitchell, Leo Monahan, Mary Monge, Larry Norton, Mindy Oliver, Darcie Park, Jon Prud'homme, Leslie Roberts, Chris Robertson, John Rowe, Larry Salk, Rob Schultz, Mike Sivak, Greg Spalenka, Lee Storey, Mia Tavanatti, Winston Taylor, Gary Tharler, Lisa Thomas, Winson Trang, Elaine Unger, Judy Unger, Brad Weinman, Don and ChaCha Weller, Brian White, Ren Wicks, Roger Xavier, Bob Young, Eddie Young.

Others who contributed: Joe Cepeda, Jamie DiSalvio, Jason Dowd, Steve Firchow, Pauline Greene, Marni Hall & Associates, Sabrina Harrison, Bill Jaynes, Mike Meyers, Paul Micich, Jo Ann Miller, Emily Rubin, Suzanne Semnacher, Bruce Schultz, Bride Whelan.

These companies donated services: American Showcase, Artworks, Graphico, The Lab, The Workbook.

SANDRA CHELIST

GARY KELLEY

"I was really wonderfully surprised when I actually saw the work on the wall. It was so different from looking at the slides."

"I was slightly surprised at the variety and quality of the very best entries. I felt the best work in the SILA show matches up very favorably to New York."

Close to finishing her master's degree in urban design at George Washington University, Sandra one day overheard a department secretary mention a new Master's Certificate program in publication design. "I was finding urban design heavy on theory," she says, "and I had always loved studio work — doing art." So she switched into GWU's Publication Specialist Design Program, and today has the enviable job of deciding how the Life & Style section of *The Los Angeles Times* looks every day. In just four years with the Times, Sandra has earned three Society of Newspaper Design awards for her art direction of the Sunday Opinion section.

Sandra learned the nuts & bolts of magazine paste-up and production with the *Armed Forces Journal* before accepting a design job with *Governing*, a lavishly printed magazine owned by the *St. Petersburg* (FL) *Times* newspaper. Then came an opportunity to join the design team at one of the world's great daily newspapers. Sandra, a St. Louis native, finds the daily deadlines of the newspaper a whole lot more rewarding than the glacial pace of urban design!

Sandra's best memory of judging day: "I had talked to Chris Payne and Gary Kelley a million times. I admire their work tremendously, and it was great to meet them. But I was just amazed to see how much Chris looks like Bill Clinton!"

Gary's stature among American illustrators can't only be gauged in gold and silver medals — like the 17 he has taken back to Iowa from the New York Society of Illustrators. Or by that same society's award for Best Illustration of the Year (1992). Or by the Ben Franklin Award from the National Booksellers Association for best illustrated youth fiction (1993). Or by similar medals, ribbons and take-home items from the Bologna (Italy) Children's Book Fair... the Society of Illustrators of Los Angeles... the New York Art Directors Club... Print Magazine... Communication Arts Magazine... the list goes on.

How many illustrators are asked, as Gary was, to paint murals, two of them, 70' in length, in Barnes & Noble's flagship book store in midtown Manhattan? He manages to keep the best of both worlds as a long-time resident of Cedar Falls, Iowa, and with an art degree from the University of Northern Iowa. Gary's distinctive and thought-provoking work has appeared in *The New Yorker, Atlantic Monthly, Time, Newsweek, Rolling Stone* and *Playboy*, and for CBS Records, the Santa Fe Opera, National Football League, and the Franklin Library.

Gary's best memory of judging day: "Finally, after hours of secret balloting, we had the refreshing and stimulating opportunity to verbalize our opinions, to agree, to disagree-and fortunately, arrive at a consensus."

editorial, book, institutional and student categories

C.F. PAYNE

"It's nice to see the inroads being made by SILA, and that there is room enough for two good national illustration shows. Anytime that we can create a forum for illustrators to show their wares and take pride in what they do, I think that benefits us all."

After graduating from Miami University at Oxford, Ohio, Chris spent the summer of 1976 at the first Illustrators Workshop. He then spent four years working in various studio jobs before beginning a freelance illustration career in 1980. He spent seven years in Dallas, where he began his long-time friendship with Art Director Fred Woodward, then returned to Cincinnati and continued to refine his unique style of illustration. He has emphasized editorial work throughout his career, but has worked on many other projects including the Popular Singers Series for the U.S. Postal Service. Chris has won numerous medals and awards from many competitions, and has had his work featured in *Communication Arts*, *American Illustration*, and the Society of Publication Designers. In the midst of this busy schedule, Chris has also found time to teach at East Texas State University, Miami University, and at Syracuse University under the direction of Murray Tinkleman.

Chris' best memory of judging day: "It was the opportunity of getting together and making new friends. We all share so much of the same things in this profession, the discussions and the camaraderie were what I enjoyed best."

LINDA WARREN

"I was generally impressed with the overall quality of this show. Viewing the work as a whole said a lot about current trends in both illustration and art direction nationally — which I found interesting in contrast to that which is happening here in Southern California."

In its first decade, The Warren Group has earned a reputation for clever, effective use of illustration in its design work. Linda especially enjoys bringing a witty, editorial style to print projects for a range of clients. These have included Mattel Toys, the University of Southern California, St. Vincent Medical Center, IVI Publishing and Harvard-Westlake School.

Linda, an Occidental College alumna, was president of the Art Director's Club of Los Angeles in 1991-93. Her work is in the Permanent Collection of the U.S. Library of Congress, and she has been honored by the AIGA, the Art Director's Clubs of Los Angeles and New York, and the American Center for Design, and others. Last year Linda also found time to earn a "Patisserie Certificate" at the formidable Ritz-Escoffier Ecole de Gastronomie Française in Paris.

Linda's best memory of judging day: "I was glad to see that I had selected or agreed with most pieces that came up in the first round of winners."

GEORGE ZEBOT

"What impressed me about the show was how different the originals looked from the slides we judged."

Professional volleyball player and coach, Peace Corps volunteer, world traveler, artist, illustrator, photographer, printmaker, teacher in four universities and institutes — George's resume can only be read in fast-forward! His illustrations, paintings, prints and photographs appear in collections from Paris to Los Angeles. George's illustration studio in Laguna Beach (near beach volleyball), provides images used in Japan, Venezuela, Mexico, and throughout the United States by such clients as CBS, the National Football League, Honda, Yamaha, Princess Cruises, and Carta Blanca.

A native of Slovenia, George came to the U.S. as a boy. His love of art led to master's degrees from both CSU Fullerton and CSU Long Beach, where he currently teaches. He is also on the art faculties at Chapman University and the University of the West Indies. His awards include a gold medal in Illustration West, an award from the New York Society of Illustrators, and similar recognition from *Communication Arts* Magazine, the Art Directors Club of New York, and *Art Direction* Magazine. George also serves on advisory boards for The Brookline Institute and the International College of Design.

George's best memory of judging day: "Judging with artists whose work I've always admired, but had never met."

editorial, book, institutional and student categories

AL ABBOTT

STEVE CHORNEY

"Overall, the show was great. I was happy to see a lot of computer art coming in."

Al's not easy to find when the weather is good. If he isn't way out there shooting car and truck commercials for his biggest client, Toyota, he's involved in Toyota's racing program. As Senior Art Director for Saatchi & Saatchi DFS Pacific, Al develops advertising campaigns for Atrigon Golf and The Skins Game, as well as various Toyota sales and recreational ventures.

Following graduation from the Art Center College of Design, Al progressed from Art Director to Creative Director to Group Head with several "name" agencies in New York and Southern California. His ideas and his artistic eye helped move products ranging from peanut butter to tires to computers. Actually, he says, the seed was planted with the "scratching and sketching" he did as a boy in very small towns in Mexico and Texas. He received a fine arts undergraduate degree from Texas A&I University before setting his sights on an advertising career. His awards include an "Addy" for his campaign for Eagle Brand Condensed Milk; an "Andy," a fistful of "Effie's" and a "Lulu" for his Toyota work. In the Illustration West show of 1989, Al was the Art Director on an award-winning illustration by Ezra Tucker for Lockheed Aeronautics.

Al's best memory of judging day: "I was amazed at how everybody still had a sense of humor after a very long day in a dark room."

"Such a wide variety of styles, and so many entries well done made the job of judging difficult."

When Steve arrived in Southern California in 1971 from upstate New York, he had a fierce determination to succeed as an artist. He got his first job in the field of art in the form of television commercial animation. This association led to numerous freelance projects and contact with other very talented artists. Without the benefit of a formal education in art, Steve nonetheless has had a highly successful freelance illustration career. He has produced the designs and poster art for numerous motion pictures, and illustrations for such clients as Disney, Universal, MGM, NBC and CBS as well as a variety of national advertising assignments.

Steve's best memory of judging day: "Working with the wonderful people at the Society of Illustrators of Los Angeles."

medical, black and white, advertising, entertainment and self-promotional/unpublished categories

GARY MEYER

"My overall impression of the show? It was that I envied the talent of all these people."

Gary has devoted a quarter-century to illustration, graphic arts and sculpture. Honors? In the Illustration West shows alone, he's taken home a Best of Show, two Gold Medals, one Silver Medal, and four special judges awards. "Firsts" abound in competitions held by the International Society of Airbrush Arts, the Springville Museum of Art, the American Society of Aviation Artists, and others. His certificates of "distinction" and "excellence" number more than 100!

An honors graduate of the Art Center College of Design, Gary has long taught perspective and illustration at the same school. His students can't get enough of Gary's technical advice — always delivered with modesty and bubbling humor. During the Korean war he served in a Marine aviation unit, and his paintings of military and civil aircraft are owned by the likes of Boeing, Lockheed and McDonnell Douglas. For virtually every major movie studio, Gary has developed backgrounds and characters — Star Wars and Supertrain are among his film credits. Gary is a native of Boonville, MO; and a past President of SILA.

Gary's best memory of judging day: "I guess it was finding out I could disagree with designers without having a fist-fight!"

KEVIN REAGAN

"The highlight was going to the show on opening night and seeing all the pieces hung. I think Picasso would've freaked!"

Kevin is the Senior Art Director at Geffen Records in Los Angeles. He has headed the department since 1989, and had been responsible for the design and advertising campaigns for releases by Guns N' Roses, Cher, Sonic Youth, Rickie Lee Jones and Pat Metheny among others. His work has won him recognition from *Print* Magazine, *Communications Arts*, the AIGA, *Billboard* Magazine, and The Type Directors Club.

Kevin's best memory of judging day: "I liked arguing with some of the other judges over which particular pieces should be recognized. You begin to feel like the artist's agent or something!"

ELLEN STEFANI

"I was very impressed with the work: a lot of varieties and styles, very professional quality."

Ellen came to Columbia Tri-Star Television in 1992 with an impressive array of design credentials. For starters, she earned "distinction" grades in graphic design as an undergraduate at San Jose State University. Then, after two years of postgraduate study at the Art Center College of Design, Ellen joined Bass/Yager & Associates, and art-directed major corporate identity programs for AT&T, General Foods and NCR. Work for clients and agencies – including her own firm, Stefani Design – included packaging, corporate identity, promotions, agency recruitment and print campaigns.

At Columbia Tri-Star, Ellen is Director of Creative Services for a new in-house agency. She is responsible for creating several award-winning advertising and promotional campaigns for first-run and off-network series, home video and motion picture packages. Ellen's work has won 18 national awards and is in the Permanent Collection of the Library of Congress. She is a native of Keokuck, Iowa.

Ellen's best memory of judging day: "It was a playful, fun time with the other judges."

medical, black and white, advertising, entertainment and self-promotional/unpublished categories

The Best of Show award is named for Joseph Morgan Henninger, a founding member of SILA over 40 years ago and its first President. At 90 years of age, he is still painting, and continues to present the fortunate recipient with his namesake award at our opening night reception.

"Joe Henninger and I have been friends ever since he was my teacher at the first Art Center, located on 7th Street in LA, when it was fast becoming the leading art school in the nation. Later, we even shared a studio in New York during the great illustration boom of the 40s, 50s and 60s."

"Joe has the gift of being able to romanticize the art of illustration, and still is one of the truly great draftsmen of our time. Joe was head of the illustration department at Art Center for 27 years, and nursed some 3,000 budding students to artistic maturity. He is an inveterate story-teller, which adds greatly to the substance of his teaching. In his distinguished career, he has run the gamut of the graphic arts in nearly every discipline, both as a performer and teacher. I am proud and happy to count him as one of my very best friends."

– Ren Wicks

The odds surely did not favor an art career for Braldt, growing up in small towns in the north tip of Holland. But his father, Jan Bralds, would bring home scraps of white cereal box board from his job in a paper mill — an innocent enough thing for a Dad to do for a little boy. "He may not have known what he was doing," recalls Braldt. "But the seed was planted ." Quietly, young Braldt would scribble away on the white scraps of cardboard, with crayons or anything handy. The imagination was working full-blast — but his parents did not catch on. He was "11 or 12," Braldt recalls, when he replied to a magazine ad for Holland's version of the Famous Artists' School. Soon he was sending samples of his drawing to his mailbox mentors. "I did it kind of sneaky," he says. "Then one day a man came to our door and told my Dad that I was talented, and that he should nurture my art career."

The elder Bralds was furious, "and embarrassed at this guy showing up at our door." Young Braldt's future lay in a respectable profession, he made clear, meaning almost anything other than art. The boy was warned never to do anything this foolish again. So three years later, Braldt sent in more samples and another Famous Artists sales rep showed up at the door. "This time Dad was really furious because I had gone against his advice." His parents, however, sensing that their son's curious talent might be an advantage in a respectable trade such as printing, sent Braldt to the Grafische School (graphics school) in Rotterdam.

As a relaxation from his schooling, Braldt would go into Holland's great art museums and draw. "I learned my craft from the resources that were available," he says. "Museums were a big influence. So were the Dutch masters, who produced such beautiful, precise work." After graduation, he took a job with an advertising agency in Rotterdam and married Charlotte, a girl from his home town. And there's a story!

Like most Dutch kids, Braldt skated the frozen canals and rivers; and when he was 12, he developed a mad crush on a skater who wore red mittens and a red scarf. A few winters in a row the two skated together but never talked. Braldt was smitten. "She disappeared when the ice was gone," he says. "I never found her again." Now fast-forward years later to a dinner party at Braldt and Charlotte's flat in Rotterdam. Braldt was telling his guests about skating with that little girl with the red scarf

and mittens. Charlotte remained strangely silent. Very quietly then she asked: "was that you who always wore the blue jacket?" Yes, it had been Charlotte out there on the ice — but Braldt had never learned who she was!

For the initial Grand Marnier campaign, Braldt prepared 10 sketches, one being the woodpecker. Braldt says "It was really amazing to work when the client just lets you go. The sketch was really just a doodle. They just looked at the doodle and said go with it." The client had so much trust in Braldt's ability, he said "I don't want to see anything in between, I just want to be surprised at the end." Adding the oranges was Braldt's idea. "I made the oranges the theme to carry throughout this campaign. Having that color was fun to work into each of the paintings." The 'visual mischief' (as Braldt calls it), in each of the six paintings was also Braldt's doing. "It wasn't planned at all in the beginning." he says, "it was just something that happened in the process and kept it interesting for me and the viewer." For the duration of the campaign, the client sent back only one painting for minor changes, the rest were used as is. Now that the client is no longer with the agency, this famous campaign has definitely ended. Does Braldt have any thoughts on that? "The freedom was exceptional, and adding the visual mischief was a treat, I felt that people don't like to look at just products, so it was nice to hear that they were looking forward to seeing the mischief in each new ad."

His masterful technique has drawn such clients as the United Nations Environment Programme, *Time, Newsweek, Rolling Stone*, the St. Louis Zoo, British Airways, and IBM. The Society of Illustrators in New York has given Braldt three Gold and three Silver awards as well as its Hamilton King Award. He has also won a Clio.

Has all this acclaim persuaded Jan Bralds, back home in Holland, that his boy chose an O.K. career path to follow after all? "I hear from others that he's proud of me, and that he's always bragging about my work," says Braldt. "But Dad never tells me."

– Bob Young

[**JOSEPH MORGAN HENNINGER AWARD · BEST OF SHOW**]

ILLUSTRATOR
BRALDT BRALDS

MEDIUM
OIL ON CANVAS

ART DIRECTOR
ARNIE ARLOW

AGENCY
TBWA ADVERTISING

CLIENT
CARILLON IMPORTERS/GRAND MARNIER

"Patrick Nagel and I first met in the early 1970s when we were both members of SILA, and we taught at Art Center on Fridays. He was a popular teacher, and influenced many of our students to go on and become successful illustrators. I remember Pat had one of the best looking cars in the school parking lot, a parking lot where fine cars got noticed!"

"Pat was one of the hardest working illustrators I've ever known, working late nights at the boards was usual. His subject was women, and his approach was simple, smooth, very designed, but most of all beautiful. And he had style, he really did have style. His fame came from this style, seen first in Playboy *magazine, then in mall poster galleries. Usually people within this industry know the names and styles of their peers, but even the general public knew Pat Nagel's name and could recognize his work immediately. He was indeed one of the few celebrity illustrators, and his fame grew even after his passing."*

— Don Weller

Balancing the ball and the brush, illustrator Mike Benny spends his time painting and playing baseball. He has a passion for both pursuits, and when he can combine them, it's an awarding-winning meld.

When he was a child, Mike loved to look at art. According to Mike, he had always been a "decent artist", and while in college determined that art was something he could make a living at. He attended California State University, Chico, where he majored in graphic design. Illustration was not a discipline the university offered, so he supplemented his design courses with painting classes and derived his own illustration projects. With the encouragement of a buddy with similar interests, he developed a portfolio of his own. In 1987, he graduated from CSU Chico, spent three years working as a graphic designer, and then launched his freelance career in 1990.

Those artists who influenced his working style were among the American regionalist painters of the nineteen thirties and forties: artists such as Thomas Hart Benton and Edward Hopper. Mike works in acrylics and sometimes layers them with oil varnishes. In developing a style of painting, he begins with a sketch, transfers it to illustration board, and begins with his brushes. "The one thing I regret in not going to art school," Mike says, " was that I missed learning better technical aspects of painting: the shortcuts, the tricks with your medium, things like that. Technically, I'm still painting the way I did when I was in school."

Mike Benny's award-winning illustration in this exhibition is a perfect example of the marriage of Mike's two passions. The painting depicts Josh Gibson, a player in the old Negro Leagues of the 1940s. The image was created as a promotional piece for the ad agency Seraphein Beyn. The agency's principal, Bob Beyn, is a good friend of Mike's, and together they share a love of baseball. The agency's motto is "Hard Hitting Advertising," and every year, Mike and Bob get together, decide on a ballplayer who epitomized strength and power, and feature the player in the promotion. Mike has 100 percent creative freedom on the project, and has been doing it for the past four years. They've already decided that next year's promotion will feature Ty Cobb.

Just mention baseball, and Mike laughs. "I just love baseball. I would rather have been a baseball player than an illustrator, it is really my illustrations that support my baseball habit." Mike actually turns down major illustration assignments to play ball and coach Little League. He says that one of the reasons he

loves baseball so much is that it's self-directed— you're competing with yourself to improve. "I'm always trying something new in baseball to improve my game." Mike claims he works on his hitting style as much as he works on his illustration style, and finds that the effort helps keep his paintings fresh. His baseball training has helped him to break out of illustration slumps, and this discipline helps to overcome road blocks when he paints.

Being single, Mike's time is currently divided equally between wielding a bat and wielding his brush. He plays in two leagues in the Sacramento area and holds batting averages of .440 in one league and .340 in the other. He enjoys coaching the Little League team, giving kids a head start, and insists "I might have been a better baseball player if I had a coach when I was a kid."

As an illustrator, Mike has painted just about every subject except for product. In the future he would like to concentrate more on the editorial markets, but is also very interested in doing entertainment art; things like rock n' roll posters and such. He is also considering doing limited edition prints— of ballplayers, of course.

Asked about the future of illustration and where he sees the profession headed, Mike comments that he hopes to see an increasing regard for illustration as art. The value of a painting created for reproduction is as significant as the use for which is was created. He sees the computer as helpful when circulating one's portfolio. Everything can be scanned onto a disk and sent out to prospective clients, and an illustrator can have dozens of floppy disk portfolios going out all over at once, thereby increasing his or her exposure. However, a computer cannot do everything, and people should soon tire of seeing photo-manipulated images. Illustration presents more options, and art buyers will soon look more to illustrators for their needs. Mike is looking forward to good things, whatever they end up being. His talents should keep him painting well and hitting well for years to come.

— Alvalyn Lundgren

ISSUES

NO MATTER WHERE YOU MAY LIVE

OR WORK, ALL ILLUSTRATORS

ARE BOUND TOGETHER BY

YOUR PROFESSION. WHEN I BEGAN TO

ASSEMBLE THIS PUBLICATION,

A PRIORITY WAS TO REACH OUT AND

PROVIDE MEANINGFUL DISCUSSIONS

FOR ALL ILLUSTRATORS NATIONWIDE,

INCLUDING THOSE WHO MAY NOT

HAVE BEEN ABLE TO ENTER,

ATTEND OR EXHIBIT IN ILLUSTRATION

WEST. TO DO THIS, I RESOLVED TO

PROVIDE A FORUM FOR PROMINENT

PEOPLE IN THIS FIELD TO

Illustration for me is more fun than it is work, like being paid to pursue my hobby with a passion. Of course, it is more than a hobby-it is a business as well-with deadlines to meet and clients to deal with. Sometimes these factors can be distracting, but always the drawing, painting and visualizing must come first.

To maintain these priorities, I have to stay motivated, stay interested. This means a continuing search for new inspiration. It means always being alert for fresh ideas, seeing and absorbing as much visual stimuli as possible, be it my environment, a bookstore, a film, a museum. The successful illustrator's mind should be a vast library of images on file. Nothing is totally original, created in a vacuum! All images are at least subliminally influenced by previous images. The key word here is 'influenced', not to be confused with 'plagiarized'. Much can be learned by studying the works of others, but, to copy that work, and call it your own, is not only illegal, it is immoral.

Ideally, influences will be adapted, edited and applied in ways that eventually culminate in an illustrator's personal vision. I've traveled through a number of influences to arrive at the illustrative statements I make in 1994. I've taken fragments from a great many sources and reorganized them to fit my own visual personality. The results have been generally satisfying, but the work needs to be constantly changing and growing. It's important for me to learn to do what I do as well as I can possibly do it, but also to move on when I get too comfortable and the work begins to stagnate. Moving on, however, does not mean following trends merely for the sake of selling more art. It means keeping in touch with your own spiritual needs as an artist and an individual, maintaining that edge that makes you feel alive in the studio.

My philosophy has always been to be true to oneself, motivated by the assignment, and not the budget. Obviously, negotiating budgets is a necessary evil of the business side of what we do, but money is only one of many factors in considering new projects. The overriding factor for me is almost always the potential joy(or lack thereof) in creating the image itself, followed by the dead-line, the exposure, and the dollars, in that order. Adhering to this philosophy is the major reason I still truly look forward to most every day in the studio.

Gary Kelley
Illustrator

Right after WWII, New York City was undisputedly the art capital of the world. Painters, sculptors, muralists, designers and illustrators were turning out work at record levels, all 35,000 of them. Magazine illustrators alone were producing 250 major story illustrations per week for women's magazines in New York, and advertisers were buying thousands of advertising illustrations, 24 sheets, labels, package designs, movie ads and annual report covers in the major advertising centers east and west. It was an art and graphics era America shall never see again.

Being lucky enough to have been around during those years, it's tough today to witness the present disintegration of the design and illustration industry. Not just fine illustration, but such impressive trades and skills as hand lettering, calligraphy, airbrush re-touching, spot designers, scratchboard artistry, pin-up artistry, industrial illustration; whole graphic industries of highly trained specialists forced out of business.

The erosion began to appear around 1965, the main culprit: television. As magazine fiction began to disappear from the magazines, so did illustration. Not only women's magazines, but sports, outdoor and car publications; magazines began to revert to their original form, the almanac. Eventually in the mid-eighties came the final blow, the emergence of the computer. It single-handedly scuttled the fine classic print, design and illustration business and its supporting industries that had developed in the first 75 years of the twentieth century, and this great trade has all but evaporated as we approach the 21st century.

Fortunately, I was able to start my career in a small studio in Los Angeles in the late thirties. Because I was the only illustrator in the studio, I was forced to learn nearly every design and painting skill and illustration technique, which probably served me well later on. It also gave me the courage to quit copying other artists, and inject my own self into my work. The two basic premises I learned back then were: A. You attack every illustration challenge, and in the process find what hidden capabilities are really inside of you, and B. you gain a true grasp of every basic discipline in drawing, perspective, composition and anatomy, each skill helping the others to refine your product. It builds a basic ethic in you that carries throughout your career.

So now, whither the art business, and illustration in particular? In the future, I see two distinct possibilities: the emerging super technologies in communications revolutionizing human relationships in the years immediately ahead, and the de-emphasizing of print and graphics of every kind, not very good for us illustrators. Or, eventually, the trend may veer away from the antiseptic technologies and impersonal electronic mediums, and the painted picture may re-establish itself as a social and historical medium. I hope that artists will continue to interpret life and make honest and perhaps romantic statements about it. After all, there are few phonies in the top echelons of the arts, because what you are as a person and an artist is right out there for everyone in the world to see, in spite of vogues and trends that may come and go. So, our job as illustrative interpreters of life is to contribute that unique something that we alone can add to the splendor of the scene around us, ourselves, that pinch of "me" belonging to the world of the painted picture.

Ren Wicks
Illustrator
SILA Founding Member
Life Achievement Honoree

"I am an illustrator. I am an illustrator."

I like the way that sounds. In fact I like all that simple statement means. That sentence may raise an inquisitive eyebrow to those who don't know what we do or understand why we do it. After describing what an illustrator is, words like fun and interesting soon follow in order to compliment you on your good fortune. Indeed, I like being in a profession that is thought of as fun and interesting. What troubles me about the use of these words in conjunction with illustration is that somehow the difficulty, dedication and devotion one has to have to be successful is lost. (I define success as being able to provide for yourself and a family if you have one.) I believe it is an affront to our profession to foster any ideas that an illustrator's dedication and work habits are less than those who happen to be an attorney, doctor, or writer. With that off my chest, let me say:

"I am so lucky to be an illustrator."

I mean it. I actually have the good fortune of having someone call me on the telephone, ask me to make a picture and offer to pay me to boot! I have been trying to draw and make good pictures since early grade school, now I get paid to do it, plus my supplies are better. It just amazes me, and I know that I am fortunate.

To work hard is easy. That may sound odd at first, but if you think for a second, it is crystal clear and makes perfect sense. You need the ability to take in the world around you, or as N.C. Wyeth said, "Be like a sponge and absorb all." Wyeth tells us to be like a sponge and absorb all around us and then wring it out once in awhile. He is telling us not to be so consumed by our goals that we forget the see the world in which we exist. If we can't see our world, how are we going to illustrate it correctly? Take your talent and all of your life experiences, childhood memories, books you've read, movies you've seen, art you've studied, 'hell-how about that sun breaking through the clouds this morning!' and use them in your work today.

Illustration is not a job, it is a career. Each project is another step, each having its own merits, its own ups and downs, each presenting new and sometimes old challenges. It is how you face these challenges and the frame of mind that you bring to it that determines the outcome. In the end you have to ask yourself just the one question: "Do I like what I'm doing?"

Being an illustrator should create more pleasure than pain. The pleasure is found in the work in front of you which is creative, substantive, informative and exciting. The pain is found with equal ease in the same place, work that can be dull, uninformed, easy. Couple that with some horrific deadline, unending changes that go nowhere, less than pleasant art directors and you have a tough day ahead of you. But therein lies your challenge. If the job seems dull, find something in the job to challenge you. Make it a value study, a color study, a fold study. Find something in that job and make it just for you. An illustration (and life as a matter of fact) has the ability to give, but only if you have the desire to seek it out. When you begin to get into the hard work is just about when the fun starts. The enjoyment that comes out of your fingertips onto the pencils, pens, paint brushes; pushing all kinds of gunk around on paper, making all kinds of neat pictures. Isn't that great? Now say it, "I like being an illustrator!"

C. F. Payne
Illustrator

Although I'm an art director, I don't believe in over-art directing. For me, the greatest control comes in letting go. Each job is a true collaboration, and I treat the artist as an equal participant. Once I sell the idea of using illustration to a client and go through the extensive process to select the right illustrator, I believe you should have the freedom to do your job. That means delivering on your style *and* creative thinking.

But being a professional means other things as well. Following these three ethical practices have benefited my career.

Keep your commitments.

If you said you'll deliver roughs on Wednesday, do it. Timeliness really is next to Godliness in this business. Set up realistic expectations in the beginning. Then I can negotiate with the printer based on when he'll get the job and not face costly delays down the line. Rule number two:

Understand how your actions impact the rest of the process.

You may create your art in splendid isolation, but it's not used that way. You're part of a team. The more you're aware of what the art director and the printer need from you– in terms of concept, mechanical requirements and time– the better. The key is to:

Communicate.

About everything. Before the job begins, that includes money, scheduling, usage and expectations. Once the job's under way, don't dramatically alter the style you've been hired for– unless you and the art director agree first. The most crucial phase may come after initial sketches are done and approved. Be very clear. About color palette; order of illustrations, if important; who's liable for corrections, and what choices you can make in terms of medium and canvas size for the best possible reproduction. And in these sensitive times, don't overlook your responsibility to consider racial and gender balance in your illustrations. It's our duty to guide clients in this important issue.

Not every job is ideal. I tell illustrators if I have money but no time, plenty of time and extra tear sheets but little money, exposure but a tight time schedule. Know your parameters and be flexible. If you and the art director communicate at each stage, you can only increase the odds of a successful project. And come through it with everyone's ethics intact.

Linda Warren
Principal
The Warren Group

I used to keep a scrapbook of images old and new and that piqued my interest creatively. Years later I had accumulated some fifteen volumes of visuals to be used for ideas and inspiration. I always felt that I needed to rely on scrap and other people's concepts to get my juices going. One day I tried to find a visual that I was remembering from one of those scrapbooks. I couldn't find it. I had collected too many images and too many scrapbooks to be able to source what I needed. Designer John Casado was in my office at the time and saw me in the midst of my dilemma. He said he'd thrown away all of his scrap and wasn't relying on it anymore. "Our minds are computers" he said, "and we are constantly in the process of storing and distilling the millions of images that our brain have taken in as a result." John's ideas that he presents to his clients, therefore, remain fresh, innovative and, above all, his own.

With the sheer number of new illustrators and designers entering the field every year, the only thing separating them from the working professional in style and concept is individuality, to be able to create their own style and process that is true to themselves. Mimicking a current style or trend will only get you temporary work and a journeyman's wage. As an art director at a record company, I'm always looking for the artist who just happens to be working as a commercial illustrator. If they are faithful to who they are, the individuality emerges.

Illustration is generally used because it is appropriate for the project and conventional photography couldn't accomplish the same results. Illustration is a visual world all its own, limited only by imagination, and we all need to push more for that land of illusion. This is a call to arms, or rather wrists that can draw and create. There is tremendous power in the image being created. No matter how decorative or conceptual, our images impart information. Therein lies the responsibility and the privilege of our craft.

Tommy Steele
Vice President, Art + Design
Capitol Records, Inc.

INSTITUTIONAL

GOLD MEDAL

JOHN ENGLISH

SILVER MEDAL

BRAD HOLLAND

BRONZE MEDAL

SERGIO BARADAT

[INSTITUTIONAL GOLD MEDAL]

ILLUSTRATOR
JOHN ENGLISH

MEDIUM
OIL

ART DIRECTOR
SHARON O'MARA

CLIENT
RAPHAEL HOTEL GROUP

I

[INSTITUTIONAL SILVER MEDAL]

ILLUSTRATOR
BRAD HOLLAND

MEDIUM
ACRYLIC ON WOODEN PANEL

ART DIRECTOR
CLAUDIA BRAMBILLA

AGENCY
J.W. THOMPSON. MILAN, ITALY

CLIENT
ANSALDO

[INSTITUTIONAL BRONZE MEDAL]

ILLUSTRATOR
SERGIO BARADAT

MEDIUM
GOUACHE & COLLAGE

ART DIRECTOR
LYNETTE CORTEZ

AGENCY
ALEXANDER ISLEY DESIGN

CLIENT
CHAMPION PAPER COMPANY

ILLUSTRATOR
MIKE BENNY

MEDIUM
ACRYLIC

AGENCY
AD F/X

CLIENT
CARLE GRIFFITH

● 4

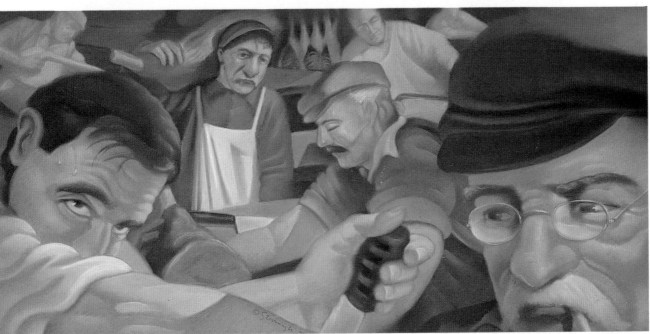

ILLUSTRATOR
MICHAEL STEIRNAGLE

MEDIUM
PASTEL

ART DIRECTOR
STEVE MUNRO

CLIENT
CHICAGO
HISTORICAL SOCIETY

● 5

INSTITUTIONAL

ILLUSTRATOR
KAZUHIKO SANO

MEDIUM
ACRYLIC

ART DIRECTOR
KAZUHIKO SANO

CLIENT
SAN FRANCISCO
SOCIETY OF
ILLUSTRATORS

● 6

ILLUSTRATOR
WILLIAM STOUT

MEDIUM
OIL ON CANVAS

ART DIRECTOR
WILLIAM STOUT &
LEX VANDERENDE

AGENCY
EXHIBITS, HOUSTON
MUSEUM OF
NATURAL SCIENCE

CLIENT
HOUSTON MUSEUM
OF NATURAL
SCIENCE

● 7 [Detail]

ILLUSTRATOR
WILLIAM STOUT

MEDIUM
OIL ON CANVAS

ART DIRECTOR
WILLIAM STOUT &
LEX VANDERENDE

AGENCY
EXHIBITS, HOUSTON
MUSEUM OF
NATURAL SCIENCE

CLIENT
HOUSTON MUSEUM
OF NATURAL
SCIENCE

● 8 [Detail]

ILLUSTRATOR
TERRY RAVANELLI

MEDIUM
MARKERS,
COLORED PENCILS

ART DIRECTOR
GRADY PHELAN

AGENCY
MARITZ, INC.

CLIENT
LITEL TELE-
COMMUNICATIONS

● 9

ILLUSTRATOR
CHRIS SHEBAN

MEDIUM
WATERCOLOR,
PENCIL, PASTEL

ART DIRECTOR
JOAN BODY

AGENCY
STUDIO GRAFIKA

CLIENT
CHARTER MEDICAL

● 10

ILLUSTRATOR
LARRY LIMNIDIS

MEDIUM
OIL ON GESSOED
PAPER

ART DIRECTOR
JAMIE MARTORANO

AGENCY
FAST FORWARD
COMMUNICATIONS

CLIENT
ACORD, THE
AGENCY

● 11

INSTITUTIONAL

ILLUSTRATOR
FRANCIS LIVINGSTON

MEDIUM
OIL & COLLAGE

ART DIRECTOR
BILL DUNN

AGENCY
WILLIAM DUNN
DESIGN

CLIENT
EXTRA SAUCE CARDS

● 12

ILLUSTRATOR
GREGORY MANCHESS

MEDIUM
OIL

ART DIRECTOR
BRAD JANSEN

CLIENT
NATIONAL FOOTBALL
LEAGUE

● 13

ILLUSTRATOR
C. MICHAEL DUDASH

MEDIUM
OIL ON LINEN

ART DIRECTOR
C. MICHAEL DUDASH
AND ANTON
TIELMANS

CLIENT
TRIAD PUBLISHING

● 14

IILLUSTRATOR
GREG SPALENKA

MEDIUM
MIXED MEDIA

ART DIRECTOR
DEANNE BUDNEY

AGENCY
CITRON, HALIGMAN,
BEDECARRÉ

CLIENT
OPEN HAND

● 15

ILLUSTRATOR
PHIL BOATWRIGHT

MEDIUM
OIL AND ACRYLIC
ON ILLUSTRATION
BOARD

ART DIRECTOR
JEFF VALZ

AGENCY
PUSKAR, GIBBON,
CHAPIN

CLIENT
BLACK EYED PEA
RESTAURANT

● 16

ILLUSTRATOR
KAZUHIKO SANO

MEDIUM
ACRYLIC

ART DIRECTOR
TONY NAGANUMA
& DARREN WONG

AGENCY
NAGANUMA
DESIGN

CLIENT
KIMOCHI INC.

● 17

INSTITUTIONAL

ILLUSTRATOR
DIRK WUNDERLICH

MEDIUM
ACRYLIC

ART DIRECTOR
FRANK ESPINOSA

AGENCY
WARNER BROTHERS
CONSUMER
PRODUCTS

CLIENT
CLEO INC.

●○ 18

ILLUSTRATOR
DEANNA GLAD

MEDIUM
WOODCUT

CLIENT
U.S. AIR FORCE

○● 19

ILLUSTRATOR
JOHN STEGER

MEDIUM
COLORED PENCIL

ART DIRECTOR
JOHN STEGER

AGENCY
MARITZ, INC.

CLIENT
ENTERPRISE
RENT-A-CAR

● 20

IILLUSTRATOR
JOHN MATTOS

MEDIUM
AIRBRUSHED INKS

ART DIRECTOR
SUNIL BHANDARI

AGENCY
HARRIS/BHANDARI
TORONTO

CLIENT
THE MOLSEN
COMPANIES

● **21**

ILLUSTRATOR
FRANK STEINER

MEDIUM
OIL ON BOARD

ART DIRECTOR
DAVE WAGNER

AGENCY
MARITZ, INC.

CLIENT
ISUZU

● 22

ILLUSTRATOR
JOHN ENGLISH

MEDIUM
MIXED MEDIA
ON BOARD

ART DIRECTOR
CARTER WEITZ

AGENCY
BAILEY LAVERMAN

CLIENT
RINGIE PRINTING

● 23

ILLUSTRATOR
GARY PENCA

MEDIUM
GOUACHE

ART DIRECTOR
GARY PENCA

CLIENT
OCEAN
SANCTUARY
PRODUCTS

● 24

ILLUSTRATOR
JAMES DIETZ

MEDIUM
OIL ON CANVAS

ART DIRECTOR
JAMES DIETZ

AGENCY
WILKES PRESS

CLIENT
HOLLIE WILKES
TRUST

● 25

ILLUSTRATOR
JAMES DIETZ

MEDIUM
OIL ON CANVAS

ART DIRECTOR
JAMES DIETZ

AGENCY
BARON PRESS

CLIENT
75TH RANGER
REGIMENT,
U.S. ARMY

● 26

ILLUSTRATOR
THOM BUTTNER

MEDIUM
INDIA INK & PASTEL

ART DIRECTOR
NANCY KREINHEDER

AGENCY
MARITZ, INC.

CLIENT
GENERAL MOTORS

●○ 27

ILLUSTRATOR
ROGER XAVIER

MEDIUM
PEN & INK,
WATERCOLOR

ART DIRECTOR
SUSAN GARLAND
FOTI

AGENCY
WHITE DESIGN

CLIENT
SOUTHERN
CALIFORNIA EDISON

○● 28

THE COLUMBIA RIVER

ILLUSTRATOR
CRAIG MAITLEN

MEDIUM
WATERCOLOR

ART DIRECTOR
CRAIG MAITLEN

AGENCY
ART FX

CLIENT
COLUMBIA RIVER
INTER-TRIBAL FISH
COMMISSION

● 29

ILLUSTRATOR
PAM-ELA HARRELSON

MEDIUM
MIXED MEDIA, 3-D

ART DIRECTOR
PAM-ELA HARRELSON

●○ **30**

ILLUSTRATOR
LUCIE ZIVNY

MEDIUM
WATERCOLOR

ART DIRECTOR
IRAJ BOZORGMEHR

CLIENT
THE BROWN
PELICAN

○● **31**

ILLUSTRATOR
DAVE MC KEAN

MEDIUM
MIXED MEDIA

ART DIRECTOR
KENT WILLIAMS

AGENCY
ALLEN SPIEGEL
FINE ARTS

CLIENT
ALLEN SPIEGEL
FINE ARTS

●○ **32**

ILLUSTRATOR
JÖZEF SUMICHRAST

MEDIUM
TRANSPARENT DYE

ART DIRECTOR
JÖZEF SUMICHRAST

CLIENT
THE ART INSTITUTE
OF CHICAGO

○● **33**

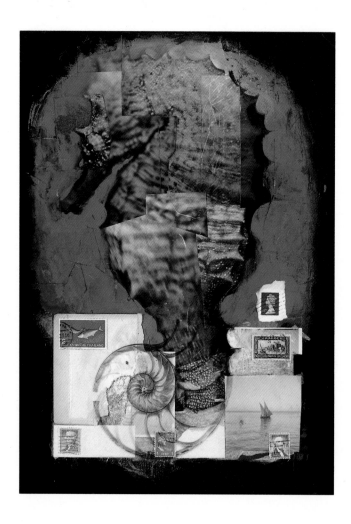

ILLUSTRATOR
C. MICHAEL DUDASH

MEDIUM
OIL ON LINEN

ART DIRECTOR
C. MICHAEL DUDASH
AND ROBERT YERKS

AGENCY
MARKETING ARTS

CLIENT
AMERICAN
EXPRESS/MARKETING
ARTS

● 34

INSTITUTIONAL

ILLUSTRATOR
BRAD HOLLAND

MEDIUM
ACRYLIC ON
WOOD PANEL

ART DIRECTOR
CLAUDIA BRAMBILLA

AGENCY
J.W. THOMPSON
MILAN, ITALY

CLIENT
ANSALDO

● **35**

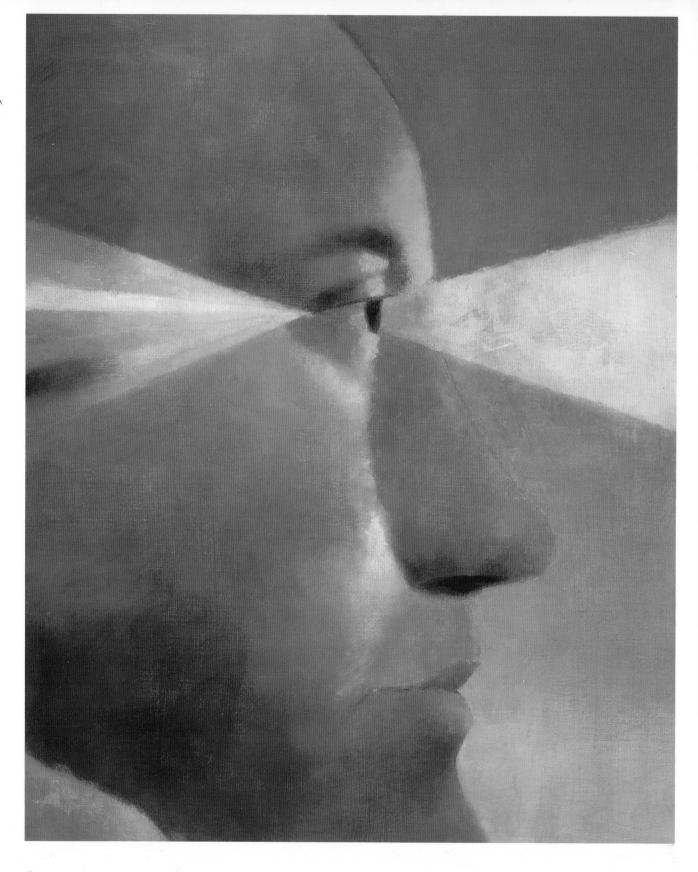

IILLUSTRATOR
CAMERON EAGLE

MEDIUM
ACRYLIC AND INK

ART DIRECTOR
LES KERR

AGENCY
KERR STARR

CLIENT
KATT RADIO
FM100,
OKLAHOMA

●○ **36**

ILLUSTRATOR
MARIA STROSTER

MEDIUM
ACRYLIC ON
BOARD

ART DIRECTOR
MARSHA ENGLE
DESIGNED BY
MARIA STROSTER

CLIENT
CLIPS, INC.

○● **37**

ILLUSTRATOR
WILLIAM O' DONNELL

MEDIUM
OIL & OIL PASTEL

ART DIRECTOR
MIKE ARTH

AGENCY
MARITZ, INC.

CLIENT
CHRYSLER

● **38**

ILLUSTRATOR
PAM-ELA HARRELSON

MEDIUM
MIXED MEDIA, 3-D

ART DIRECTOR
LORI HILDEBRAND

AGENCY
HILDEBRAND & ROSS

CLIENT
EASTRIDGE MALL

● 39

ILLUSTRATOR
JOHN MATTOS

MEDIUM
AIRBRUSHED INKS

ART DIRECTOR
J. LINEBERGER BELSER

AGENCY
GREENFIELD/BELSER

CLIENT
BZL

●○ 40

ILLUSTRATOR
TERRI STARRETT

MEDIUM
COMPUTER
GENERATED

AGENCY
PIERCE + KAUFMAN
ASSOCIATES

CLIENT
CAPITAL RESEARCH

○● 41

ILLUSTRATOR
ROGER XAVIER

MEDIUM
PEN & INK,
WATERCOLOR

ART DIRECTOR
SUSAN GARLAND
FOTI

AGENCY
WHITE DESIGN

CLIENT
SOUTHERN
CALIFORNIA EDISON

●○ 42

ILLUSTRATOR
KRISTEN
WETTERHAHN

MEDIUM
SILK SCREEN

ART DIRECTOR
KRISTEN
WETTERHAHN

○● 43

INSTITUTIONAL

ILLUSTRATOR
KERNE ERICKSON

MEDIUM
ACRYLIC

ART DIRECTOR
JANE SOBCZAK

AGENCY
BURNHARDT,
FUDYMA

CLIENT
TANA GRAPHICS

● 44

ILLUSTRATOR
KERNE ERICKSON

MEDIUM
ACRYLIC

ART DIRECTOR
JANE SOBCZAK

AGENCY
BURNHARDT,
FUDYMA

CLIENT
TANA GRAPHICS

● 45

INSTITUTIONAL

ILLUSTRATOR
PHIL BOATWRIGHT

MEDIUM
OIL & ACRYLIC
ON ILLUSTRATION
BOARD

ART DIRECTOR
DAVID BELL

AGENCY
KRAUSE AND
YOUNG

CLIENT
PRESBYTERIAN
HOSPITAL

● **50**

ILLUSTRATOR
BILL MAYER

MEDIUM
AIRBRUSH

ART DIRECTOR
FRANK GRUBLICK

AGENCY
LAUGHING DOG
STUDIO

CLIENT
LAUGHING DOG
STUDIO

● 51

ILLUSTRATOR
BILL JAYNES

MEDIUM
INK,
WATERCOLOR &
CRAYON

ART DIRECTOR
DON DAME

AGENCY
WEE WILLIE WORKS

CLIENT
TREND PACIFIC, INC.

● 52

ILLUSTRATOR
BRALDT BRALDS

MEDIUM
OIL ON MASONITE

ART DIRECTOR
DAVID BARTELS

AGENCY
BARTELS &
CARSTENS

CLIENT
ST. LOUIS ZOO

● 53

ADVERTISING

GOLD MEDAL

BILL MAYER

SILVER MEDAL

JOHN MATTOS

BRONZE MEDAL

BILL MAYER

[ADVERTISING GOLD MEDAL]

ILLUSTRATOR
BILL MAYER

MEDIUM
AIRBRUSH

ART DIRECTOR
DON SMITH

AGENCY
ADSMITH

CLIENT
HOPPER PAPER

ILLUSTRATOR
JERRY LOFARO

MEDIUM
ACRYLICS

ART DIRECTOR
KRISTINE PALLAS

CLIENT
BROWN & CADWELL

● 61

ILLUSTRATOR
BRALDT BRALDS

MEDIUM
OIL ON CANVAS

ART DIRECTOR
ARNIE ARLOW

AGENCY
TBWA ADVERTISING

CLIENT
CARILLON
IMPORTERS/GRAND
MARNIER

● 62

ILLUSTRATOR
JERRY LOFARO

MEDIUM
ACRYLICS

ART DIRECTOR
SCOTT BROOKS

AGENCY
Q1
COMMUNICATIONS

CLIENT
ARIEL, INC.

● 63

ILLUSTRATOR
BRAD HOLLAND

MEDIUM
OIL ON PANEL

ART DIRECTOR
MAUREEN KENNY

AGENCY
BERNSTEIN REIN
ADVERTISING

CLIENT
SAM'S CLUB

● 64

ILLUSTRATOR
BRALDT BRALDS

MEDIUM
OIL ON CANVAS

ART DIRECTOR
ARNIE ARLOW

AGENCY
TBWA ADVERTISING

CLIENT
CARILLON
IMPORTERS/GRAND
MARNIER

●○ 65

ILLUSTRATOR
DANILO GONZALEZ

MEDIUM
ACRYLIC

ART DIRECTOR
BOB PASCAL

AGENCY
INTET ADVERTISING

CLIENT
TREE TOP

○● 66

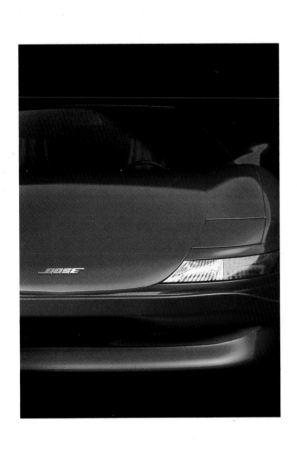

ILLUSTRATOR
MICHAEL
SCARAMOZZINO

MEDIUM
3D COMPUTER
RENDERING

ART DIRECTOR
DON LUTKUS

AGENCY
BOSE CORPORATION
AND DREAMLIGHT

CLIENT
BOSE CORPORATION

●○ 67

ILLUSTRATOR
MICHAEL SCHWAB

MEDIUM
SCREEN PRINT

ART DIRECTOR
BILL NAEGELE

CLIENT
LORD FLETCHERS

○● 68

ILLUSTRATOR
BRALDT BRALDS

MEDIUM
OIL ON CANVAS

ART DIRECTOR
ARNIE ARLOW

AGENCY
TBWA ADVERTISING

CLIENT
CARILLON
IMPORTERS/GRAND
MARNIER

● 69

ILLUSTRATOR
BRAD HOLLAND

MEDIUM
ACRYLIC ON
WOODEN PANEL

ART DIRECTOR
GUY MARINO

AGENCY
MERKLEY,
NEWMAN, HARTY

CLIENT
BANKER'S TRUST

● 70

IILLUSTRATOR
BRYAN HAYNES

MEDIUM
ACRYLIC

ART DIRECTOR
NICLAUS ZOLLER

AGENCY
LEON HARDT
& KERN

CLIENT
DIE TEPPICH GALERIE

● 71

ILLUSTRATOR
CARLOS TORRES

MEDIUM
ACRYLIC ON
ILLUSTRATION
BOARD

ART DIRECTOR
KEVIN MILLER

AGENCY
DUVAL, WOGLOM,
BRUECKNER &
PARTNERS

CLIENT
NHC
COMMUNICATIONS

● 72

ILLUSTRATOR
BRAD HOLLAND

MEDIUM
ACRYLIC ON
WOODEN PANEL

ART DIRECTOR
GUY MARINO

AGENCY
MERKLEY,
MEWMAN, HARTY

CLIENT
BANKERS TRUST
COMPANY

● **73**

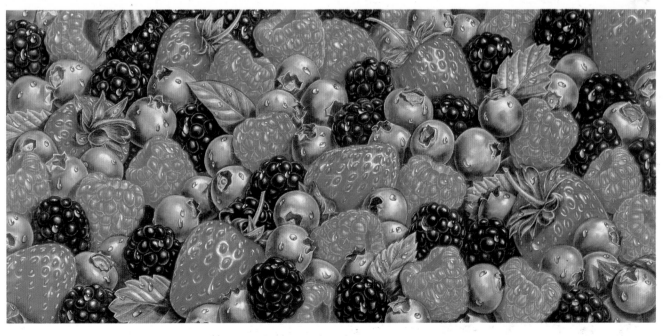

ILLUSTRATOR
DELRO ROSCO

MEDIUM
WATERCOLOR

ART DIRECTOR
ROLANDO ROSLER

AGENCY
PRIMO ANGELI

CLIENT
CRYSTAL GEYSER

● **74**

ILLUSTRATOR
DOUGLAS FRASER

MEDIUM
ALKYD ON PAPER

ART DIRECTOR
GREG RODITSKI

AGENCY
MCCAFFREY &
COMPANY

CLIENT
ASTRA/MERCK GROUP

● 75

ILLUSTRATOR
EZRA TUCKER

MEDIUM
ACRYLIC ON BOARD

ART DIRECTOR
RON LOPEZ

AGENCY
DUNN, REBER,
GLENN, MARZ

CLIENT
MGM GRAND HOTEL

● **76**

ILLUSTRATOR
GREGORY MANCHESS

MEDIUM
OIL

ART DIRECTOR
MATT REINHARD

AGENCY
FOOTE, CONE
& BELDING

CLIENT
COORS COMPANY

● **77**

IILLUSTRATOR
BRALDT BRALDS

MEDIUM
OIL ON CANVAS

ART DIRECTOR
ARNIE ARLOW

AGENCY
TBWA ADVERTISING

CLIENT
CARILLON
IMPORTERS/GRAND
MARNIER

● **81**

ILLUSTRATOR
BRAD HOLLAND

MEDIUM
ACRYLIC ON
WOODEN PANEL

ART DIRECTOR
GUY MARINO

AGENCY
MERKLEY
MEWMAN HARTY

CLIENT
BANKERS TRUST
COMPANY

● **82**

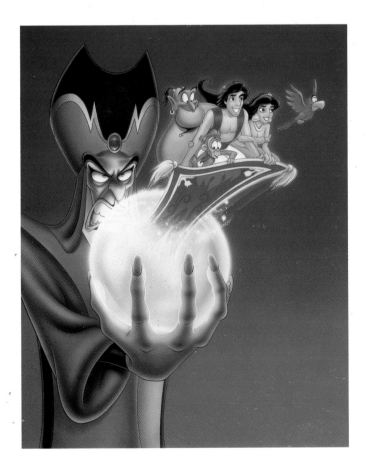

EDITORIAL

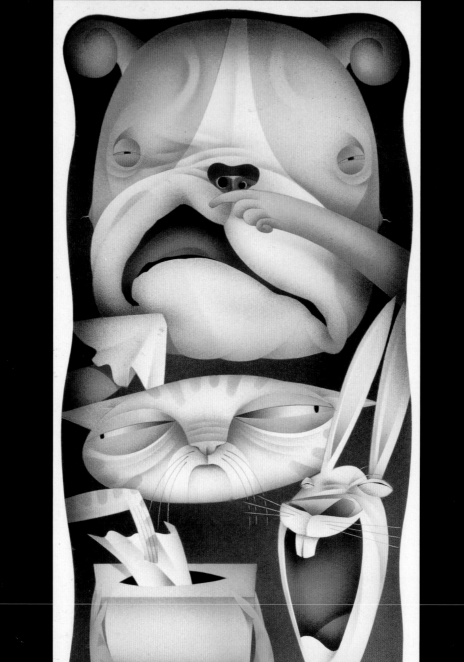

ILLUSTRATOR
GARY TAXALI

MEDIUM
ALKYD ON MASONITE

ART DIRECTOR
CHRIS NEYEN

CLIENT
PENTHOUSE
MAGAZINE

● 90

ILLUSTRATOR
TOM GARRETT

MEDIUM
COLLAGE

ART DIRECTOR
JUDY GARLAND

CLIENT
ATLANTIC
MONTHLY

● 91

ILLUSTRATOR
GREG SPALENKA

MEDIUM
MIXED MEDIA

ART DIRECTOR
TRICIA MCGINTY

CLIENT
NEW WOMAN
MAGAZINE

● 92

ILLUSTRATOR
DON ASMUSSEN

MEDIUM
PEN & INK COLLAGE

ART DIRECTOR
DOLORES MOTICHKA

CLIENT
THE WASHINGTON
TIMES

● 93

ILLUSTRATOR
FRANCIS LIVINGSTON

MEDIUM
OIL

ART DIRECTOR
CHRIS CURRY

CLIENT
NEW YORKER
MAGAZINE

● 94

ILLUSTRATOR
BILL MAYER

MEDIUM
AIRBRUSH

ART DIRECTOR
GARY BURNLOEHR

CLIENT
FLORIDA TREND
MAGAZINE

● 95

ILLUSTRATOR
JAMES ENDICOTT

MEDIUM
WATERCOLOR

ART DIRECTOR
WENDY RONGA

CLIENT
PREVENTION
MAGAZINE

● 96

EDITORIAL

ILLUSTRATOR
PETE SPINO

MEDIUM
GOUACHE &
COLORED PENCIL

ART DIRECTOR
BILL GASPARD

CLIENT
THE SAN DIEGO
UNION - TRIBUNE

● 97

ILLUSTRATOR
DOUG BOWLES

MEDIUM
PASTEL

CLIENT
PENTHOUSE
MAGAZINE

● 98

ILLUSTRATOR
CARTER GOODRICH

MEDIUM
COLORED PENCIL
AND WATERCOLOR

ART DIRECTOR
STEVE CONNATSER

CLIENT
PRIVATE CLUBS
MAGAZINE

● 99

ILLUSTRATOR
CALEF BROWN

MEDIUM
OIL & ACRYLIC
ON BOARD

ART DIRECTOR
STEPHANIE BIRDSONG

CREATIVE DIRECTOR
KATHY NENNEKER

CLIENT
SHAPE MAGAZINE

●○ 100

ILLUSTRATOR
KAREN STOLPER

MEDIUM
ACRYLIC
ON WATERCOLOR
PAPER

ART DIRECTOR
CAROL PORTER

CLIENT
THE WASHINGTON
POST

○● 101

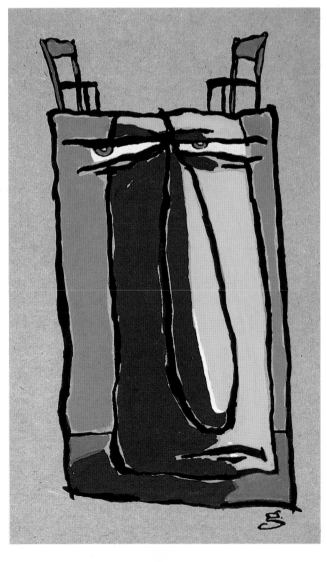

ILLUSTRATOR
BRALDT BRALDS

MEDIUM
OIL ON PAPER

ART DIRECTOR
D.J. STOUT

CLIENT
TEXAS MONTHLY
MAGAZINE

●○ 102

ILLUSTRATOR
COURTNEY GRANNER

MEDIUM
GOUACHE

ART DIRECTOR
RICHARD LEEDS

CLIENT
KEYBOARD
MAGAZINE

○● 103

ILLUSTRATOR
KAZUHIKO SANO

MEDIUM
ACRYLIC

ART DIRECTOR
RENETA WOODBURY

AGENCY
DIABLO
PUBLICATIONS

CLIENT
DIABLO ART
MAGAZINE

● 104

ILLUSTRATOR
BILL MAYER

MEDIUM
AIRBRUSH

ART DIRECTOR
ANDREA HEMMAN

CLIENT
SEVEN ARTS
MAGAZINE

● 105

ILLUSTRATOR
LISA MANNING

MEDIUM
AIRBRUSHED
ACRYLIC

ART DIRECTOR
SUZANNE MORIN

AGENCY
NATIONAL
AUDUBON SOCIETY

CLIENT
AUDUBON
MAGAZINE

● 106

ILLUSTRATOR
JUDITH REED

MEDIUM
FLASHE ACRYLICS
WITH INK OVERLAY

ART DIRECTOR
CAROL H. ROSE

CLIENT
HEINLE & HEINLE
PUBLISHING

● 107

ILLUSTRATOR
COURTNEY GRANNER

MEDIUM
INK & WATERCOLOR

ART DIRECTOR
NANCY CUTLER

CLIENT
NEW MEDIA
MAGAZINE

● 108

EDITORIAL

ILLUSTRATOR
DON ASMUSSEN

MEDIUM
PEN, INK,
WATERCOLOR &
COLLAGE

ART DIRECTOR
MATTHEW SACHUK

CLIENT
THE FIFTH
ESTATE INC.

● 109

ILLUSTRATOR
JOE SORREN

MEDIUM
ACRYLIC

ART DIRECTOR
JOE SORREN
& JOE MITCH

CLIENT
TRANSWORLD
SNOWBOARDING
MAGAZINE

● 110

ILLUSTRATOR
PAUL ROGERS

MEDIUM
ACRYLIC

ART DIRECTOR
FRED FEHLAU

CLIENT
PLAYBOY

●○ 111

ILLUSTRATOR
MARIA RENDON

MEDIUM
WOOD AND
MIXED MEDIA

ART DIRECTOR
JAY PETROW

CLIENT
BUSINESS WEEK
MAGAZINE

○● 112

ILLUSTRATOR
TIM O'BRIEN

MEDIUM
OIL ON BOARD

ART DIRECTOR
KEN SMITH

CLIENT
TIME MAGAZINE

●○ 113

ILLUSTRATOR
DON ARDAY

MEDIUM
ELECTRONIC

ART DIRECTOR
MARK GEER

AGENCY
GEER DESIGN

CLIENT
MEMORIAL
HEALTHCARE SYSTEM

○● 114

ILLUSTRATOR
JOE CEPEDA

MEDIUM
MIXED MEDIA

ART DIRECTOR
BRUCE OLSON

CLIENT
HEALTHCARE
FORUM MAGAZINE

●○ 115

IILLUSTRATOR
HAYES HENDERSON

MEDIUM
OIL

ART DIRECTOR
MARK GEER

AGENCY
GEER DESIGN

CLIENT
CARING MAGAZINE

○● 116

ILLUSTRATOR
SCOTT LAUMANN

MEDIUM
ACRYLIC & PASTEL

ART DIRECTOR
NANCY
DUCKWORTH

CLIENT
LOS ANGELES TIMES
MAGAZINE

●○ 117

IILLUSTRATOR
MARIA RENDON

MEDIUM
FOAM, MIXED MEDIA

ART DIRECTOR
NANCY CUTLER

CLIENT
NEW MEDIA
MAGAZINE

○● 118

ILLUSTRATOR
BILL MAYER

MEDIUM
AIRBRUSH

ART DIRECTOR
JOHN LYLE
SANFORD

CLIENT
DISCOVERY
MAGAZINE

● 119

ILLUSTRATOR
GREG SPALENKA

MEDIUM
MIXED MEDIA

ART DIRECTOR
PETER MORANCE

CLIENT
AMERICAN
HERITAGE MAGAZINE

● 120

ILLUSTRATOR
GUY WOLEK

MEDIUM
MIXED MEDIA

ART DIRECTOR
BOB FERNANDES

CLIENT
AMERICAN BAR
ASSOCIATION

● 121

EDITORIAL

ILLUSTRATOR
ROB CLAYTON

MEDIUM
ACRYLIC & INK
ON PAPER

ART DIRECTOR
STEPHANIE BIRDSONG

CREATIVE DIRECTOR
KATHY NENNEKER

CLIENT
SHAPE MAGAZINE

● 122

ILLUSTRATOR
PETE SPINO

MEDIUM
MIXED MEDIA

ART DIRECTOR
BILL GASPARD

CLIENT
THE SAN DIEGO
UNION - TRIBUNE

● 123

ILLUSTRATOR
DON WOOD

MEDIUM
ACRYLIC

ART DIRECTOR
CAROLITA FEIRING

CLIENT
THE PRESS ENTERPRISE

● 124

ILLUSTRATOR
DAVE CUTLER

MEDIUM
ACRYLIC ON
WATERCOLOR
PAPER

ART DIRECTOR
WENDY RONGA

CLIENT
PREVENTION
MAGAZINE

● 125

ILLUSTRATOR
FRANCIS LIVINGSTON

MEDIUM
OIL

ART DIRECTOR
CHRIS CURRY

CLIENT
NEW YORKER
MAGAZINE

● 126

ILLUSTRATOR
MARIA RENDON

MEDIUM
WOOD,
MIXED MEDIA

ART DIRECTOR
CHRISTOPHER
RAMIREZ

CLIENT
SALUDOS HISPANOS
MAGAZINE

● 127

ILLUSTRATOR
PHIL BOATWRIGHT

MEDIUM
OIL AND ACRYLIC
ASSEMBLAGE

ART DIRECTOR
LAURIE SHATTUCK

CLIENT
VIRTUE MAGAZINE

● **128**

EDITORIAL

ILLUSTRATOR
BRENT WATKINSON

MEDIUM
OIL ON CANVAS

ART DIRECTOR
MEG BIRNBAUM

CLIENT
COOKS ILLUSTRATED
MAGAZINE

● 132

ILLUSTRATOR
GARY TAXALI

MEDIUM
ALKYD ON
MASONITE

ART DIRECTOR
KRISTI ANDERSON

CLIENT
UTNE READER

● 133

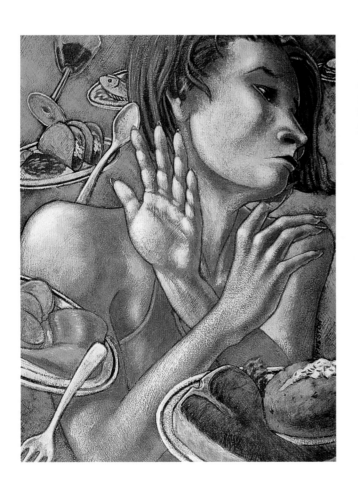

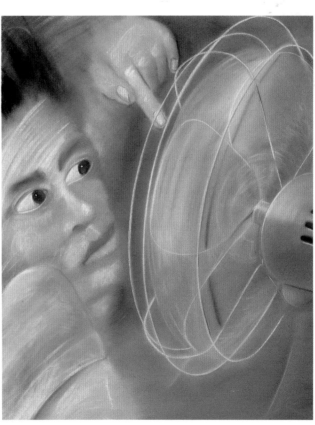

ILLUSTRATOR
R. M. KATO

MEDIUM
GOUACHE

ART DIRECTOR
KERRY TREMAIN

CLIENT
MOTHER JONES
MAGAZINE

●○ 134

ILLUSTRATOR
VICTORIA KANN

MEDIUM
COLLAGE,
MIXED MEDIA

ART DIRECTOR
KRISTI ANDERSON

CLIENT
UTNE READER

○● 135

ILLUSTRATOR
JEFF PRESTON

MEDIUM
ACRYLIC

ART DIRECTOR
RHONDA WILSON

CLIENT
AMERICAN FITNESS
MAGAZINE

●○ 136

ILLUSTRATOR
MIKE MEYERS

MEDIUM
PASTEL

ART DIRECTOR
GREG CARANNANTE

CLIENT
SUN-SENTINEL
COMPANY

○● 137

ILLUSTRATOR
STEVE KROPP

MEDIUM
OIL, COLORED
PENCIL, ACRYLIC

ART DIRECTOR
DAVID HUGHES

AGENCY
WILLIAMS &
ROCKWOOD

CLIENT
UTAH BUSINESS
MAGAZINE

● **138**

ILLUSTRATOR
BRAD HOLLAND

ART DIRECTOR
KAREN JOAJOCA
& DAN BARRON

CLIENT
ART DIRECTION
MAGAZINE

● 142

ILLUSTRATOR
COURTNEY GRANNER

MEDIUM
MIXED

ART DIRECTOR
LAURA CIROLIA

CLIENT
DIABLO MAGAZINE

● 143

ILLUSTRATOR
PHIL BOATWRIGHT

MEDIUM
OIL AND
ACRYLIC ON
ILLUSTRATION BOARD

ART DIRECTOR
SPENCER GRAHL

AGENCY
PUCKETT GROUP

CLIENT
MOODY MAGAZINE

●   144

ILLUSTRATOR
DAVID GROVE

MEDIUM
GOUACHE &
ACRYLIC ON GESSO

ART DIRECTOR
MIKE CHRISTENSEN

CLIENT
LEADERSHIP
CENTER MAGAZINE

● 145

ILLUSTRATOR
DON ASMUSSEN

MEDIUM
PEN & INK COLLAGE

ART DIRECTOR
DOLORES MOTICHKA

CLIENT
THE WASHINGTON
TIMES

●○ 146

ILLUSTRATOR
BOB YOUNG

MEDIUM
PEN AND INK
DRAWING
OVER ACRYLIC

ART DIRECTOR
MARY WEBSTER

CLIENT
DATABASE
PROGRAMMING
& DESIGN

○● 147

ILLUSTRATOR
FRANCIS LIVINGSTON

MEDIUM
OIL

ART DIRECTOR
CHRIS CURRY

CLIENT
NEW YORKER
MAGAZINE

● 148

ILLUSTRATOR
PHIL BOATWRIGHT

ART DIRECTOR
CARLA FRANK

MEDIUM
OIL, ACRYLIC &
COLLAGE ON
PLYWOOD

AGENCY
CARLA FRANK
DESIGN

CLIENT
BALTIMORE
SYMPHONY

●○ 149

ILLUSTRATOR
MIKE CRESSY

MEDIUM
MIXED MEDIA

ART DIRECTOR
DONNA BANATO

CLIENT
AV VIDEO

○● 150

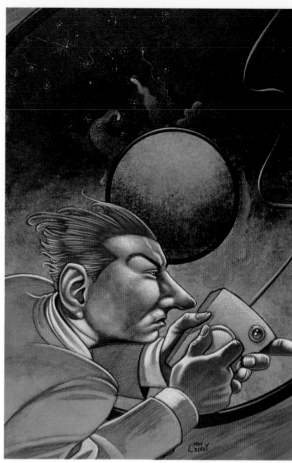

ILLUSTRATOR
BILL MAYER

MEDIUM
AIRBRUSH

ART DIRECTOR
CATHY CACCHIONE

CLIENT
AUDIO MAGAZINE

●○ 151

ILLUSTRATOR
BRYN BARNARD

MEDIUM
OIL

ART DIRECTOR
KIM MOHAN

CLIENT
AMAZING STORIES
MAGAZINE

○● 152

EDITORIAL

ILLUSTRATOR
DAN JONES

MEDIUM
PENCIL, AIRBRUSH,
COLORED PENCIL

ART DIRECTOR
ROGER DOWD

CLIENT
MEDICAL
ECONOMICS
MAGAZINE

● 153

ILLUSTRATOR
JOHN DYKES

MEDIUM
MIXED MEDIA

ART DIRECTOR
KENNETH B. SMITH

CLIENT
TIME MAGAZINE

● 154

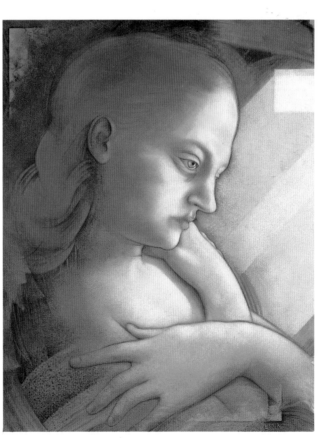

ILLUSTRATOR
BILL MAYER

MEDIUM
AIRBRUSH

ART DIRECTOR
D.J. STOUT

CLIENT
TEXAS MONTHLY
MAGAZINE

●○ 155

ILLUSTRATOR
COURTNEY GRANNER

MEDIUM
MIXED MEDIA

ART DIRECTOR
RICHARD LEEDS

CLIENT
KEYBOARD
MAGAZINE

○● 156

ILLUSTRATOR
ROBERT CRAWFORD

MEDIUM
ACRYLIC

ART DIRECTOR
SUSAN MCCLELLAN

CLIENT
HARROWSMITH
COUNTRY LIFE

●○ 157

ILLUSTRATOR
LINA CHESAK

MEDIUM
OIL & PENCIL

ART DIRECTOR
DEB FENTRESS

CLIENT
AMERICAN DIABETES
ASSOCIATION

○● 158

ILLUSTRATOR
GARY BASEMAN

MEDIUM
ACRYLIC ON
CANVAS

ART DIRECTOR
STEPHANIE
BIRDSONG

CREATIVE DIRECTOR
KATHY NENNEKER

CLIENT
SHAPE MAGAZINE

● 159

ILLUSTRATOR
HIROKO SANDERS

MEDIUM
MIXED MEDIA

ART DIRECTOR
HIROKO SANDERS

CLIENT
SUNSET TV ART
COMPANY

● 160

EDITORIAL

ILLUSTRATOR
FRANCIS LIVINGSTON

MEDIUM
OIL

ART DIRECTOR
ED SUTHRO

AGENCY
ED GUTHRO DESIGN

CLIENT
COFFY
COMMUNICATIONS

● 161

EDITORIAL

ILLUSTRATOR
DON ASMUSSEN

MEDIUM
PEN & INK COLLAGE

ART DIRECTOR
BILL GASPARD

CLIENT
THE SAN DIEGO
UNION-TRIBUNE

● 162

ILLUSTRATOR
BRAD WEINMAN

MEDIUM
OIL ON PAPER

ART DIRECTOR
JOHN D'ANGONA

CLIENT
LOS ANGELES TIMES
MAGAZINE

● 163

EDITORIAL

ILLUSTRATOR
GREG SPALENKA

MEDIUM
MIXED MEDIA

ART DIRECTOR
SANDRA EISERT

CLIENT
WEST MAGAZINE

● 164

BOOK

RICHARD ANDRI

SILVER MEDAL

REBECCA J. LEER

BRONZE MEDAL

BRAD WEINMAN

[BOOK SILVER MEDAL]

ILLUSTRATOR
REBECCA J. LEER

[**BOOK BRONZE MEDAL**]

ILLUSTRATOR
BRAD WEINMAN

MEDIUM
OIL ON PAPER

ART DIRECTOR
VAUGHN ANDREWS

CLIENT
HARTCOURT BRACE & COMPANY

ILLUSTRATOR
DON WELLER

MEDIUM
WATERCOLOR &
COLORED PENCIL

ART DIRECTOR
LUCILLE
CHOMOWITZ

AGENCY
THE WELLER
INSTITUTE FOR THE
CURE OF DESIGN

CLIENT
SIMON & SCHUSTER

● 168

ILLUSTRATOR
DICK COLE

MEDIUM
WATERCOLOR

ART DIRECTOR
SARAH HUDSON

AGENCY
TIME-WARNER
SUNSET PUBLISHING

CLIENT
SUNSET MAGAZINE

● 169

ILLUSTRATOR
CARTER GOODRICH

MEDIUM
COLORED PENCIL
AND WATERCOLOR

ART DIRECTOR
WENDY BASS

CLIENT
MACMILLAN
PUBLISHING

● 170

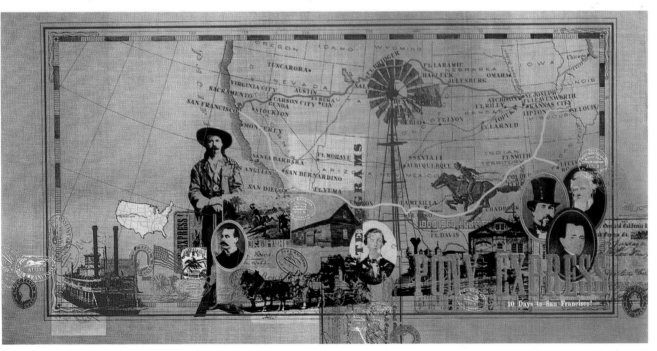

ILLUSTRATOR
TROY HOWELL

MEDIUM
PASTEL

ART DIRECTOR
DIANNE HESS

CLIENT
SCHOLASTIC, INC.

●○ 171

ILLUSTRATOR
TROY HOWELL

MEDIUM
PASTEL

ART DIRECTOR
DIANNE HESS

CLIENT
SCHOLASTIC, INC.

○● 172

ILLUSTRATOR
TED WRIGHT

MEDIUM
OIL AND COLLAGE

ART DIRECTOR
TED WRIGHT

AGENCY
MARITZ, INC.

CLIENT
UNITED STATES
POSTAL MUSEUM

● 173

ILLUSTRATOR
TOM KASPERSKI

MEDIUM
OIL

ART DIRECTOR
ELIZABETH PARISI &
MADALINA STEFAN

CLIENT
SCHOLASTIC, INC.

●○ 174

ILLUSTRATOR
TOM KASPERSKI

MEDIUM
OIL

ART DIRECTOR
ELIZABETH PARISI &
MADALINA STEFAN

CLIENT
SCHOLASTIC, INC.

○● 175

ILLUSTRATOR
THOMAS L. FLUHARTY

MEDIUM
PASTEL

● 176

ILLUSTRATOR
ROBERT RODRIGUEZ

MEDIUM
ACRYLIC,
OIL CRAYON &
PRISMACOLOR

ART DIRECTOR
MARIETTA
ARIASTASSATOS

CLIENT
DELL PUBLISHING

● 177

ILLUSTRATOR
JÖZEF SUMICHRAST

MEDIUM
TRANSPARENT DYE

ART DIRECTOR
BARBARA LEFF

AGENCY
BALLANTINE
ART DEPT.

CLIENT
RANDOM HOUSE

● 178

ILLUSTRATOR
CARTER GOODRICH

MEDIUM
COLORED PENCIL
AND WATERCOLOR

ART DIRECTOR
ALISON LEW

CLIENT
W.H. FREEMAN &
COMPANY PUBLISHERS

●○ 179

ILLUSTRATOR
WENDELL MINOR

MEDIUM
WATERCOLOR

ART DIRECTOR
NEIL ERICKSON

CLIENT
HARPERCOLLINS
PUBLISHERS

○● 180

ILLUSTRATOR
EUGENE HOFFMAN

MEDIUM
RUSTED METAL,
PRINTERS PLATES,
NAILS, WOOD

ART DIRECTOR
EUGENE HOFFMAN

CLIENT
UNIVERSITY OF
NORTHERN
COLORADO

●○ 181

ILLUSTRATOR
SERGE MICHAELS

MEDIUM
GOUACHE

ART DIRECTOR
SERGE MICHAELS

CLIENT
ENTRE D'MODE

○● 182

ILLUSTRATOR
JERRY LOFARO

MEDIUM
ACRYLIC

ART DIRECTOR
GEORGE
CORNWELL

CLIENT
NEW AMERICAN
LIBRARY

● **183**

ILLUSTRATOR
TROY HOWELL

MEDIUM
GOUACHE,
PASTEL, GOLD LEAF,
MARBLEIZED PAPER

ART DIRECTOR
RON MCCUTCHAN

CLIENT
CRICKET MAGAZINE

●○ 184

ILLUSTRATOR
CAROL NEWSOM

MEDIUM
ACRYLIC

ART DIRECTOR
PATTI ESLINGER

CLIENT
TROLL ASSOCIATES

○● 185

ILLUSTRATOR
RAFAL OLBINSKI

MEDIUM
ACRYLIC ON
CANVAS

ART DIRECTOR
MARTHA PHILIPS

CLIENT
FRANKLIN LIBRARIES

● 186

ILLUSTRATOR
WENDELL MINOR

MEDIUM
WATERCOLOR

ART DIRECTOR
SUZANNE NOLI

CLIENT
HARPERCOLLINS
PUBLISHERS

●○ 187

ILLUSTRATOR
JOHN THOMPSON

MEDIUM
ACRYLIC

ART DIRECTOR
CLAIRE COUNIHAN

CLIENT
SCHOLASTIC, INC.

○● 188

ILLUSTRATOR
ROBERT RODRIGUEZ

MEDIUM
ACRYLIC &
PRISMACOLOR

ART DIRECTOR
GEORGE CALAS

CLIENT
READER'S DIGEST
CONDENSED
BOOKS

● 189

ILLUSTRATOR
JOHN THOMPSON

MEDIUM
ACRYLIC

ART DIRECTOR
CLAIRE COUNIHAN

CLIENT
SCHOLASTIC, INC.

● 190

ILLUSTRATOR
MARC BURCKHARDT

MEDIUM
ACRYLIC

ART DIRECTOR
ANDY CARPENTER

AGENCY
BURCKHARDT
STUDIO

CLIENT
RANDOM HOUSE

●○ 191

ILLUSTRATOR
LEE MACLEOD

MEDIUM
ACRYLIC

ART DIRECTOR
RICK TELANDER

CLIENT
RICK TELANDER

○● 192

ILLUSTRATOR
MARC BURCKHARDT

MEDIUM
ACRYLIC

ART DIRECTOR
MARIO PULICE

AGENCY
BURCKHARDT
STUDIO

CLIENT
DOUBLEDAY
PUBLISHING

● 193

ILLUSTRATOR
WILLIAM STOUT

MEDIUM
PEN, BRUSH, INK
ON STRATHMORE
BRISTOL

ART DIRECTOR
WILLIAM STOUT
& LEN BROWN

CLIENT
TOPPS COMICS, INC.

● 194

ILLUSTRATOR
THOM ANG

MEDIUM
MIXED MEDIA

ART DIRECTOR
FRED SCHILLER

AGENCY
ALLEN SPIEGEL
FINE ARTS

CLIENT
ECLIPSE BOOKS

●○ 195

ILLUSTRATOR
MARK BISCHEL

MEDIUM
OIL

ART DIRECTOR
DEA MARKS

AGENCY
GREG & ASSOCIATES

CLIENT
PERFECTION
LEARNING

○● 196

ILLUSTRATOR
ROBERT RODRIGUEZ

MEDIUM
ACRYLIC, OIL &
PRISMACOLOR

ART DIRECTOR
GERALD COUNIHAN

CLIENT
DELL PUBLISHING

● 197

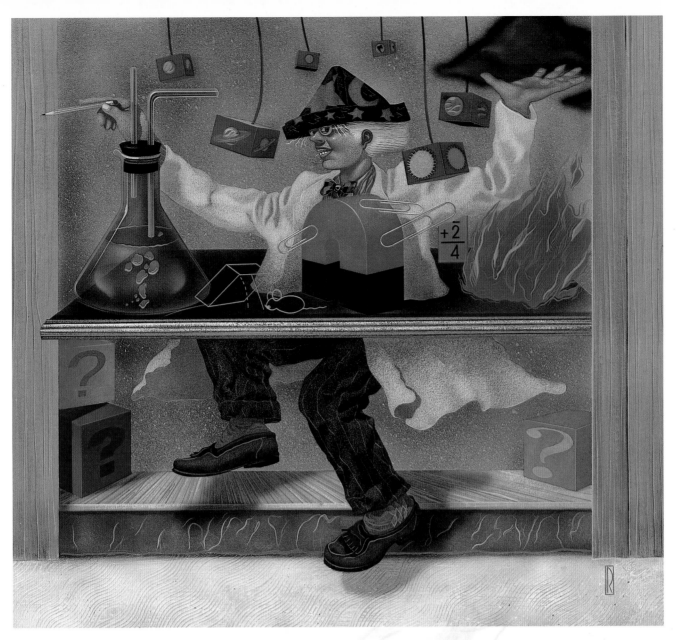

ILLUSTRATOR
RUBEN RAMOS

MEDIUM
ACRYLIC &
COLORED PENCIL

ART DIRECTOR
STEPHANIE MOTZ

CLIENT
ENCYCLOPEDIA
BRITANNICA

● 198

ILLUSTRATOR
ROBERT MEGANCK

MEDIUM
GOUACHE

ART DIRECTOR
TOBY SCHMIDT

AGENCY
COMMUNICATION
DESIGN, INC.

CLIENT
RUNNING PRESS
BOOK PUBLISHERS

● 199

ILLUSTRATOR
TOM GARRETT

MEDIUM
COLLAGE

ART DIRECTOR
CRAIG YOE

CLIENT
MATTEL

● **200**

ILLUSTRATOR
ROBERT RODRIGUEZ

MEDIUM
ACRYLIC, OIL &
PRISMACOLOR

ART DIRECTOR
BRAD JANSEN

AGENCY
N.F.L. PROPERTIES

CLIENT
N.F.L. PROPERTIES &
TURNER PUBLISHING

●○ 201

ILLUSTRATOR
SERGIO BARADAT

MEDIUM
GOUACHE

ART DIRECTOR
MARIO DULICE

CLIENT
DOUBLEDAY BOOKS

○● 202

ILLUSTRATOR
CHRIS HOPKINS

MEDIUM
OIL

ART DIRECTOR
BRAD JANSEN

CLIENT
N.F.L. PROPERTIES

● 203

ILLUSTRATOR
WENDELL MINOR

MEDIUM
WATERCOLOR

ART DIRECTOR
MARIETTA
ANASTASSATOS

CLIENT
DELL PUBLISHING

● 204

ILLUSTRATOR
WINSON TRANG

MEDIUM
ACRYLIC

ART DIRECTOR
WINSON TRANG

CLIENT
GAMMONTON
GRAPHICS

● 205

ILLUSTRATOR
VIRGINIA HALSTEAD

MEDIUM
OIL STICK, OIL
PASTEL ON PAPER

ART DIRECTOR
VIRGINIA HALSTEAD

AGENCY
SARA SMITH
DESIGNE

CLIENT
ALGONQUIN
BOOKS OF
CHAPEL HILL

●○ 206

ILLUSTRATOR
DOUG BOWLES

MEDIUM
PASTEL

ART DIRECTOR
DEBBIE GOLDBECK

CLIENT
DOUBLEDAY BOOKS

○● 207

ILLUSTRATOR
RUBEN RAMOS

MEDIUM
ACRYLIC &
COLORED PENCIL

ART DIRECTOR
STEPHANIE MOTZ

CLIENT
ENCYCLOPEDIA
BRITANNICA

●   208

ILLUSTRATOR
JOHN THOMPSON

MEDIUM
ACRYLIC

ART DIRECTOR
CLAIRE COUNIHAN

CLIENT
SCHOLASTIC, INC.

● 209

ILLUSTRATOR
ROBERT RODRIGUEZ

MEDIUM
ACRYLICS,
GOUACHE,
CRAYONS,
PRISMACOLOR

ART DIRECTOR
LESLIE OSHER

CLIENT
PRENTICE HALL

● 210

ILLUSTRATOR
REBECCA J. LEER

MEDIUM
PASTEL

ART DIRECTOR
LUCILLE
CHOMOWICZ

CLIENT
SIMON & SCHUSTER

● 211

BLACK & WHITE

GOLD MEDAL

JEFF GEORGE

SILVER MEDAL

ROGER XAVIER

BRONZE MEDAL

SALLY MORROW

ILLUSTRATOR
ROGER XAVIER

MEDIUM
SCRATCHBOARD

ART DIRECTOR
RON ROMAN

AGENCY
ALTMAN MEDER LAWRENCE HILL

CLIENT
GTE TELECOMMUNICATIONS SERVICES

ILLUSTRATOR
IRENA ROMAN

MEDIUM
GRAPHITE

ART DIRECTOR
LISA RICHMOND

CLIENT
BERKSHIRE MAGAZINE

●○ 215

ILLUSTRATOR
MIKE HODGES

MEDIUM
ALKYDS ON PAPER

ART DIRECTOR
DAVID JOHNSON

AGENCY
UNIVERSITY OF
MIAMI MAGAZINE

CLIENT
UNIVERSITY OF MIAMI

○● 216

P A R K

C I T Y

P A R K

C I T Y

ding branches of the aspen, and the snow, which bombarded us just last week, is now a distant vision on the skyline. Ribbons of irrigation canals feed the surrounding pastures. Everywhere we hear the drone of tractors and watch flocks of seagulls following each farmer's water turn.

MAY 25. The change of seasons is like a tug of war in the winds. One minute we are reading in a lawn chair, the sun hanging in a tranquil sky, when suddenly a breeze flips the page. A rogue thunderhead slides over the ridge; the horizon darkens and dust-filled winds sweep through the valley. Ranchers rush in from the fields on spooked horses whinnying and shying from the flying debris. With the wind a familiar scent filters into town. It is the nostril-searing smell of branding season: of bellowing cattle, singed hair and hide mixed with fresh-trampled hay and manure.

JUNE 11. Cowboys and cattle are on the move toward summer pastures. We hear the cattle drive approaching like the honking of a distant traffic jam. Everyone rushes to close garden gates so the herd won't be tempted to stop for a snack, while baffled summer visitors fume behind the wheels of overheated campers. In the evening, we listen to the ruckus of a pajama-league softball game and dodge past piles of bicycles left helter-skelter in the street. After a long winter of home-work and hibernation, the neighborhood posse

has returned to chase frogs in the irrigation ditch, float bottle caps down the creek and spend nickels at the cash store's penny candy department.

JUNE 30. Each breeze sends a cloud of cotton-wood seeds parachuting down from the old trees by the river. The dogs are sneezing and the pond is covered with layers of this summer snow. The seeds flutter down, skitter across the road, get tangled in our eyelashes and tickle the backs of our throats. In the forest the snow has retreated from our favorite summer trails, revealing a bright bouquet of wildflower-filled meadows. Miniature elephanthead and delicate monkey flowers line the path, while a pair of Western tanagers beam orange and yellow flashes

through the pines.

JULY 4. The whole town turns out for the parade down Main and Center. Lawn chairs and tailgates unfold just after daybreak as generations of locals take up traditional posts. There are "howdys" and "look-how-he's-grown-up" pats all around no politics today, no cynicism or protest, just small-town

patriotism. While floats of dairy princesses, veterans, rodeo clowns and baton twirlers strut by, we are for the moment part of the American ideal.

JULY 16. Local ranchers are rushing to harvest the first cut of alfalfa, which lies in contoured rows throughout the valley. Farm machines

ka-chunk through-out the long night, leaving behind a trail of twine-wrapped hay bales. Haywagons weave down the highway with a precarious circus of kids and dogs

frolicking on top. For a month everyone has been trying to grab summer by the horns and bulldog it to the ground. Toy-laden campers head for the high country to bicycle, fish, hike, and build campfires, while sailors and waterskiers breeze across the reservoirs. The trout are biting in Crooked Creek and hummingbirds dive-bomb each other for prime perches on the feeder.

JULY 29. A record-breaking 88-degree afternoon sends us squinting for shade. The dogs are panting, flowers wilt, and life at the ranch slows to a halt. Horses gather in the shade, tails rhyth-mically swat flies while their owners loi-ter at the cash store sipping sodas. Pickup trucks on the back road leave a jet trail of dust, and giant wheels of irrigation sprinklers are working overtime. Thunderheads rumble and kick up dust devils, but their cargo evaporates in the hot air before reaching parched brown pastures.

AUGUST 3. The harvest has begun: sweet peas off the vine, too many radishes, a colorful row of deep red and yellow beets, several varieties of lettuce, spinach, onions, com-frey, kohlrabi and carrots. Instead of standing in line at the market we spend the evenings rinsing homegrown bounty at the water pump. The garden, at this point, bears little resemblance to the well-ordered plan we laid out last spring. Errant potato

ILLUSTRATOR
DON WELLER

MEDIUM
INK AND
TYPESETTING

ART DIRECTOR
DON WELLER

AGENCY
THE WELLER
INSTITUTE FOR THE
CURE OF DESIGN

CLIENT
MERIDIAN
INTERNATIONAL

● 217

BLACK AND WHITE

ILLUSTRATOR
JEFF GEORGE

MEDIUM
PEN & INK

ART DIRECTOR
MAYA METZ

AGENCY
SLAUGHTER HANSON
ADVERTISING

CLIENT
UNITED CHAIR
COMPANY

● 218

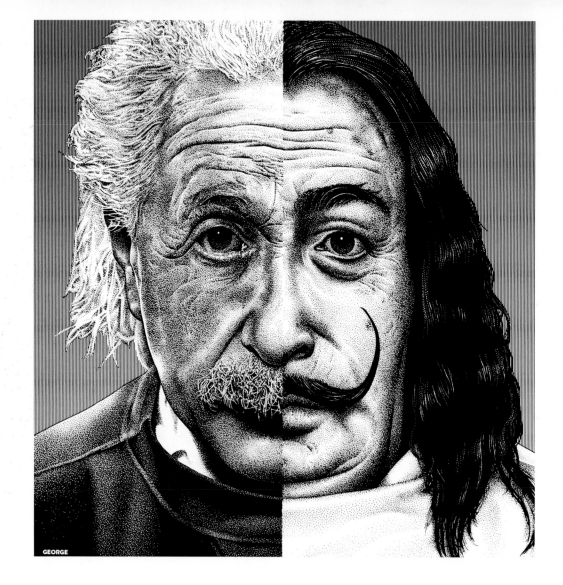

ILLUSTRATOR
DON WELLER

MEDIUM
INK

ART DIRECTOR
DON WELLER

AGENCY
THE WELLER
INSTITUTE FOR THE
CURE OF DESIGN

CLIENT
MERIDIAN
INTERNATIONAL

● 219

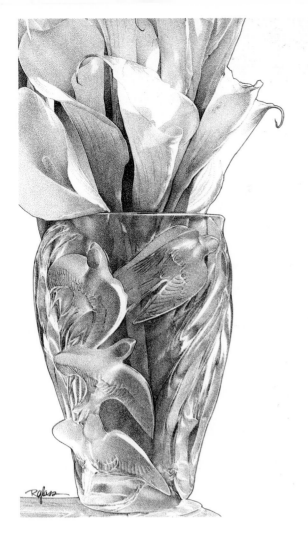

ILLUSTRATOR
RANDY GLASS

●○ 220

ILLUSTRATOR
DON ASMUSSEN

MEDIUM
PEN & INK COLLAGE

ART DIRECTOR
DIANA CHANTICK

CLIENT
THE LOS
ANGELES TIMES

○● 221

ILLUSTRATOR
ALAN CARR

MEDIUM
ALKYD ON PAPER

● 222

ENTERTAINMENT

GOLD MEDAL

ROBERT RISKO

SILVER MEDAL

JEFF WACK

BRONZE MEDAL

MARIA STROSTER

ILLUSTRATOR
STEVE MILLER

MEDIUM
COLORED PENCIL &
OIL PASTEL

ART DIRECTOR
RIKKI POULOS

AGENCY
RIKKI POULOS
DESIGN

CLIENT
NATIONAL
ACADEMY OF
RECORDING ARTS &
SCIENCE

● 226

ILLUSTRATOR
CHERIE BENDER

MEDIUM
OIL ON CANVAS

ART DIRECTOR
CHERIE BENDER

AGENCY
FARFALLA
ILLUSTRATION

CLIENT
FIRST IMPRESSIONS

● 227

ENTERTAINMENT

ILLUSTRATOR
SAHAK EKSHIAN

MEDIUM
COMPUTER,
PHOTOSHOP

ART DIRECTOR
BRIAN WEINER &
SAHAK EKSHIAN

AGENCY
THE ILLUSION
FACTORY

CLIENT
CINEMA AWARDS

●○ 228

ILLUSTRATOR
ROGER MOTZKUS

MEDIUM
ACRYLIC &
PRISMACOLOR

ART DIRECTOR
VU TRAN

AGENCY
30/SIXTY DESIGN

CLIENT
PARAMOUNT HOME
VIDEO

○● 229

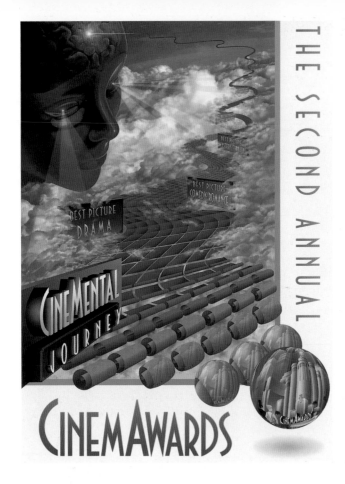

ILLUSTRATOR
EDDIE YOUNG

MEDIUM
ACRYLICS

ART DIRECTOR
LIZ DAVIS

CLIENT
KIDSGUIDE

○● 230

ILLUSTRATOR
DAN GOOZEE

MEDIUM
ACRYLIC

ART DIRECTOR
BOB RODGERS

AGENCY
BRC IMAGINATION
ART

CLIENT
KNOTTS BERRY
FARM

○● 231

ENTERTAINMENT

ILLUSTRATOR
LORRAINE MASCHLER

MEDIUM
ACRYLIC

ART DIRECTOR
LYNE WALKER

AGENCY
GRAPHIC
PRODUCTIONS

CLIENT
THE LAGUNA
PLAYHOUSE

● 232

ILLUSTRATOR
FRANCIS LIVINGSTON

MEDIUM
OIL

ART DIRECTOR
JAN DANFORTH

AGENCY
TERRY PIMSLER

● **235**

ILLUSTRATOR
BRAD WEINMAN

MEDIUM
OIL ON PAPER

ART DIRECTOR
FRED FEHLAU

CLIENT
PLAYBOY

● **236**

ILLUSTRATOR
LARRY SALK

MEDIUM
ACRYLIC ON
ILLUSTRATION
BOARD

ART DIRECTOR
DAVID FOSTER

CLIENT
READYSOFT, INC.

●○ 237

ILLUSTRATOR
ROBERT RISKO

MEDIUM
GOUACHE

ART DIRECTOR
TOMMY STEELE

AGENCY
CAPITOL RECORDS
ART DEPT.

CLIENT
CAPITOL RECORDS,
INC.

○● 238

ILLUSTRATOR
DIRK WUNDERLICH

MEDIUM
AIRBRUSH

ART DIRECTOR
DIRK WUNDERLICH

CLIENT
AMERICAN
SOFTWORKS
CORPORATION

● 239

ENTERTAINMENT

ILLUSTRATOR
ROBERT RISKO

MEDIUM
GOUACHE

ART DIRECTOR
TOMMY STEELE

AGENCY
CAPITOL RECORDS
ART DEPT.

CLIENT
CAPITOL RECORDS,
INC.

● 240

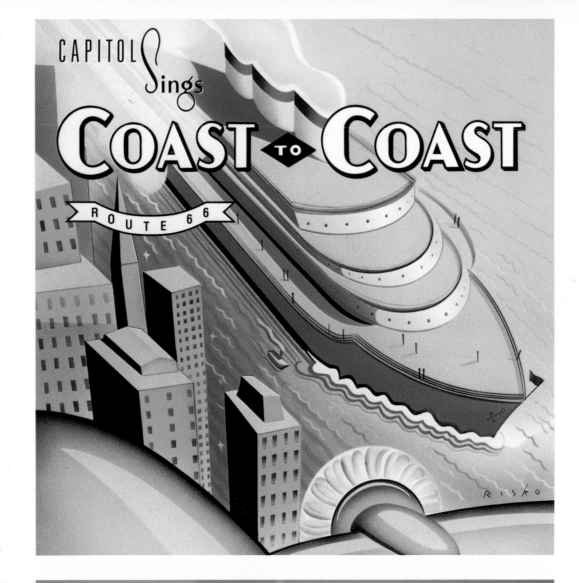

ILLUSTRATOR
ROBERT RISKO

MEDIUM
GOUACHE

ART DIRECTOR
TOMMY STEELE

AGENCY
CAPITOL RECORDS
ART DEPT.

CLIENT
CAPITOL RECORDS,
INC.

● 241

ILLUSTRATOR
ROBERT RODRIGUEZ

MEDIUM
ACRYLIC,
CRAYONS &
PRISMACOLOR

ART DIRECTOR
HOWARD FRITZON

CLIENT
SONY

● 242

SELF-PROMOTIONAL/ UNPUBLISHED

GOLD MEDAL

DAVID BOWERS

SILVER MEDAL

BRYN BARNARD

BRONZE MEDAL

BRAD WEINMAN

WEINMAN

ILLUSTRATOR
MARTHA ANNE
BOOTH

MEDIUM
OIL PASTEL ON
PAPER

● 246

ILLUSTRATOR
LEE
MACLEOD

MEDIUM
ACRYLIC

● 247

SELF-PROMOTIONAL/
UNPUBLISHED

ILLUSTRATOR
MIKE BENNY

MEDIUM
ACRYLIC

● 248

ILLUSTRATOR
C. MICHAEL DUDASH

MEDIUM
OIL ON CANVAS

● 249

IILLUSTRATOR
ROBERT JEW

MEDIUM
ACRYLIC
ON CANVAS

● 250

**SELF-PROMOTIONAL/
UNPUBLISHED**

ILLUSTRATOR
GREGORY MANCHESS

MEDIUM
OIL

● 253

ILLUSTRATOR
PAUL ALEXANDER

MEDIUM
GOUACHE

● 254

SELF-PROMOTIONAL/
UNPUBLISHED

IILLUSTRATOR
GREG TUCKER

MEDIUM
PASTEL

ART DIRECTOR
RICK VAUGHN

AGENCY
WEDEEN CREATIVE

CLIENT
BECKETT PAPER
COMPANY

● 255

ILLUSTRATOR
RICHARD LAURENT

MEDIUM
OIL ON CANVAS

●○ 256

ILLUSTRATOR
HERB MOTT

MEDIUM
OIL ON CANVAS

○● 257

ILLUSTRATOR
EUGENE HOFFMAN

MEDIUM
TWIGS, PAPER,
PAINT

● 258

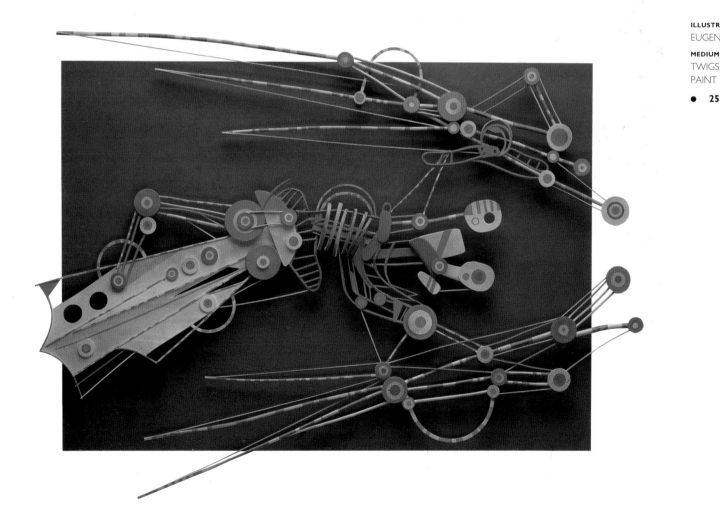

ILLUSTRATOR
JOHN ENGLISH

MEDIUM
OIL ON CANVAS

ART DIRECTOR
SHARON O'MARA

AGENCY
RAPHAEL HOTEL
GROUP

● **259**

ILLUSTRATOR
DAN
GOOZEE

MEDIUM
PASTEL

●○ 260

ILLUSTRATOR
JIMMY HOLDER

MEDIUM
WATERCOLOR

○● 261

ILLUSTRATOR
DAVID HALEY

MEDIUM
WATERCOLOR

ART DIRECTOR
DAVID HALEY

AGENCY
MARITZ, INC.

CLIENT
CHRYSLER

● 262

SELF-PROMOTIONAL/
UNPUBLISHED

ILLUSTRATOR
THOMAS L. FLUHARTY

MEDIUM
PASTEL

● 263

ILLUSTRATOR
RICHARD ADKINS

MEDIUM
AIRBRUSH, ACRYLIC,
COLORED PENCIL

● 264

ILLUSTRATOR
MARTHA ANNE
BOOTH

MEDIUM
OIL PASTEL ON
PASTEL CLOTH

● **269**

ILLUSTRATOR
DOUG BOWLES

MEDIUM
PASTEL

ART DIRECTOR
BET DAVID

CLIENT
RICHARD SALZMAN

● **270**

SELF-PROMOTIONAL/
UNPUBLISHED

ILLUSTRATOR
LISA FRENCH

MEDIUM
ACRYLIC

● 272

ILLUSTRATOR
WAYNE GALLIPOLI

MEDIUM
OIL ON MASONITE

● 273

SELF-PROMOTIONAL/
UNPUBLISHED

IILLUSTRATOR
JOHN THOMPSON

MEDIUM
ACRYLIC ON
WOOD

CLIENT
NEW JERSEY
COUNCIL ON THE
ARTS

● 274

 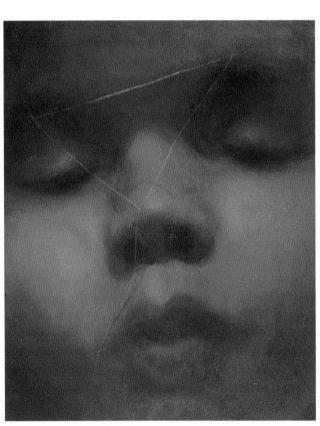

ILLUSTRATOR
JAEEUN CHOI

MEDIUM
ACRYLIC

ART DIRECTOR
SUNGHEE HAHN

CLIENT
JAE & HAHN DESIGN

● 275

ILLUSTRATOR
VIDAL CENTENO

MEDIUM
ACRYLIC ON PAPER

●○ 277

ILLUSTRATOR
MARK H. ADAMS

MEDIUM
GOUACHE

○● 278

ILLUSTRATOR
KEVIN CARMONA

MEDIUM
ACRYLIC & OIL

●○ 279

ILLUSTRATOR
ROBERT BURGER

MEDIUM
GOUACHE

○● 280

ILLUSTRATOR
CARLOS TORRES

MEDIUM
ACRYLIC ON
ILLUSTRATION
BOARD

● 281

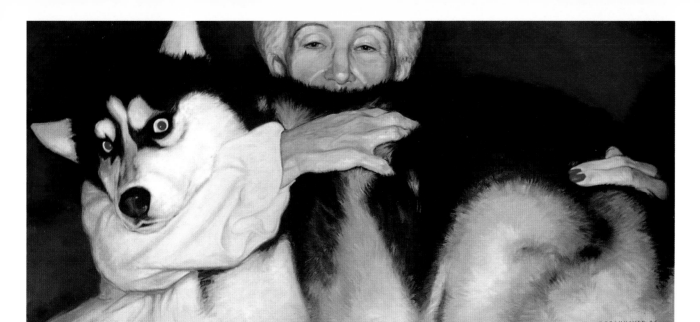

ILLUSTRATOR
TREVOR COPENHAVER

MEDIUM
OIL ON CANVAS

● 282

ILLUSTRATOR
TIM O'BRIEN

MEDIUM
OIL ON BOARD

● 283

ILLUSTRATOR
LISA VALENTI

MEDIUM
INK & PASTEL

●○ 284

ILLUSTRATOR
ELISSÉ JO GOLDSTEIN

MEDIUM
WATERCOLOR

○● 285

ILLUSTRATOR
COLIN POOLE

MEDIUM
OIL

ART DIRECTOR
SAL BARRACCA
& COLIN POOLE

●○ 286

ILLUSTRATOR
TED COCONIS

○● 287

ILLUSTRATOR
DAVID BOWERS

MEDIUM
OIL ON MASONITE

● 288

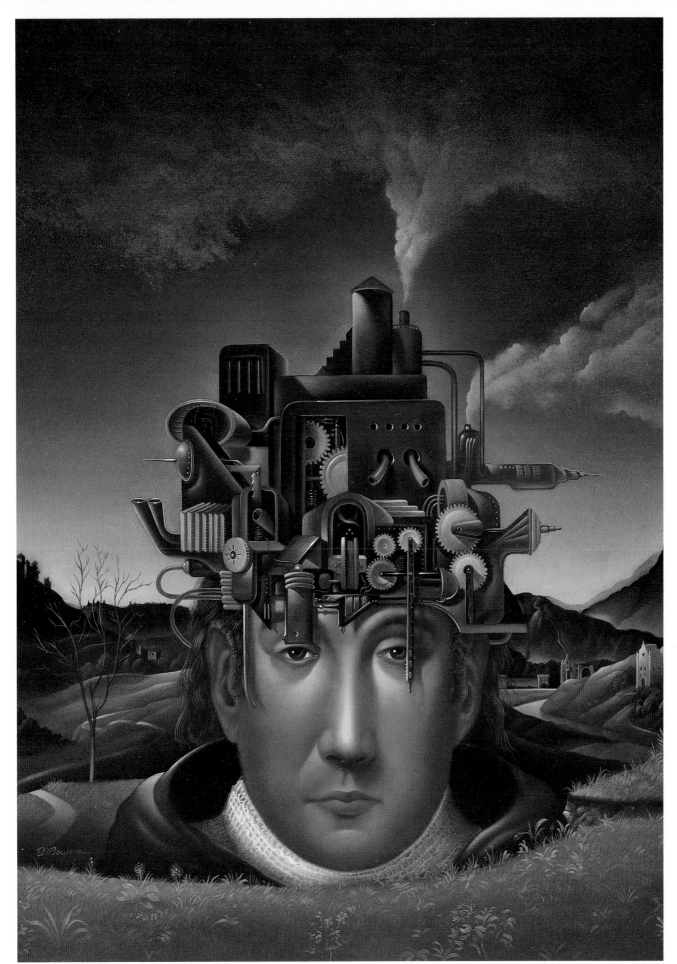

**SELF-PROMOTIONAL/
UNPUBLISHED**

ILLUSTRATOR
KEN ROSENBERG

MEDIUM
ACRYLIC

○● 291

ILLUSTRATOR
DIANA FRITCH

MEDIUM
OIL

○● 292

ILLUSTRATOR
BOB COMMANDER

MEDIUM
ACRYLIC & OIL

●○ 293

ILLUSTRATOR
DAVID PILAND

MEDIUM
MIXED MEDIA

○● 294

SELF-PROMOTIONAL/
UNPUBLISHED

ILLUSTRATOR
LISA FRENCH

MEDIUM
ACRYLIC

● **295**

ILLUSTRATOR
PAULINE GREENE

MEDIUM
COLORED PENCIL,
PASTEL, INK
TRANSFER, WASH

●○ 296

ILLUSTRATOR
PETER
HEER

MEDIUM
ACRYLIC, METAL
FLAKE, LACQUER

○● 297

ILLUSTRATOR
STEPHEN MAGSIG

MEDIUM
COLLAGE

● 298

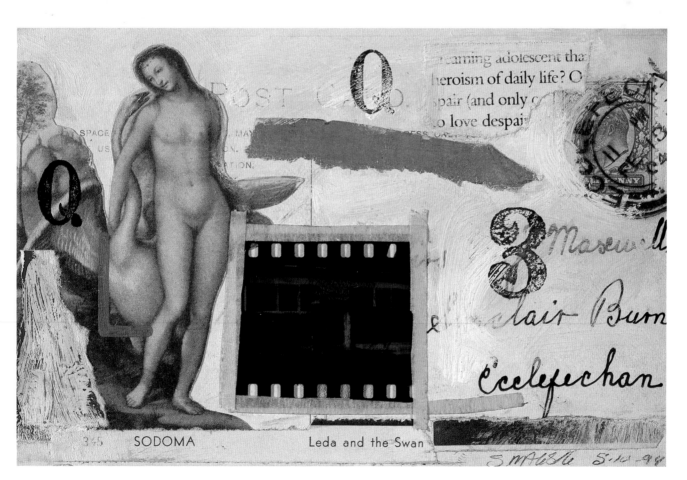

SELF-PROMOTIONAL/
UNPUBLISHED

ILLUSTRATOR
ROBERT BURGER

MEDIUM
GOUACHE

● 302

**SELF-PROMOTIONAL/
UNPUBLISHED**

ILLUSTRATOR
CRAIG SIMPSON

MEDIUM
WATERCOLOR &
COLORED PENCIL

●○ 303

ILLUSTRATOR
LISA MANNING

MEDIUM
AIRBRUSHED
ACRYLICS

ART DIRECTOR
CRAIG YOE

AGENCY
CRAIG YOE STUDIOS

CLIENT
MATTEL TOYS

○● 304

ILLUSTRATOR
SCOTT ANGLE

MEDIUM
ACRYLIC

● 305

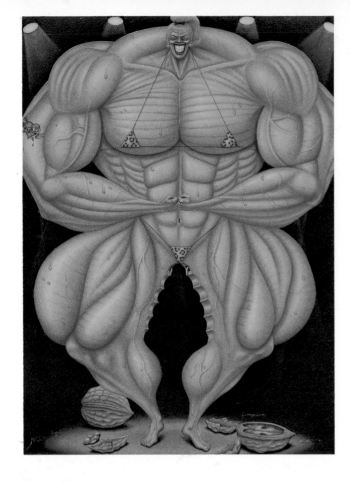

ILLUSTRATOR
BYRON COONS

MEDIUM
ACRYLIC & PENCIL
ON ILLUSTRATION
BOARD

● 306

ILLUSTRATOR
MICHAEL THORNTON

MEDIUM
ACRYLIC ON
ILLUSTRATION
BOARD

ART DIRECTOR
JACKI THORNTON

● **307**

ILLUSTRATOR
TERRY KOVALCIK

MEDIUM
AIRBRUSH &
WATERCOLOR

● **308**

ILLUSTRATOR
DON ARDAY

MEDIUM
ELECTRONIC

● **309**

SELF-PROMOTIONAL/
UNPUBLISHED

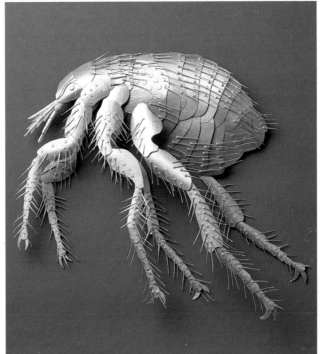

ILLUSTRATOR
LESLIE ROBERTS

MEDIUM
COLORED PENCIL

●○ 310

IILLUSTRATOR
EUGENE HOFFMAN

MEDIUM
MIXED MEDIA

○● 311

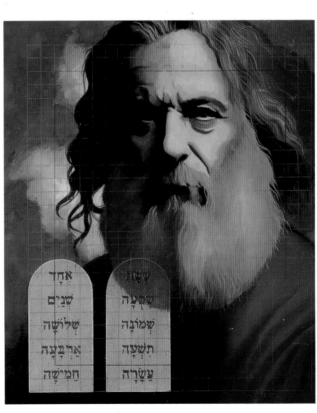

IILLUSTRATOR
FRANCES
MIDDENDORF

MEDIUM
GOUACHE AND INK

●○ 312

ILLUSTRATOR
STEVEN WOLFGANG

MEDIUM
OIL, GOUACHE &
INK ON BOARD

○● 313

ILLUSTRATOR
GARY PENCA

MEDIUM
GOUACHE

● 317

**SELF-PROMOTIONAL/
UNPUBLISHED**

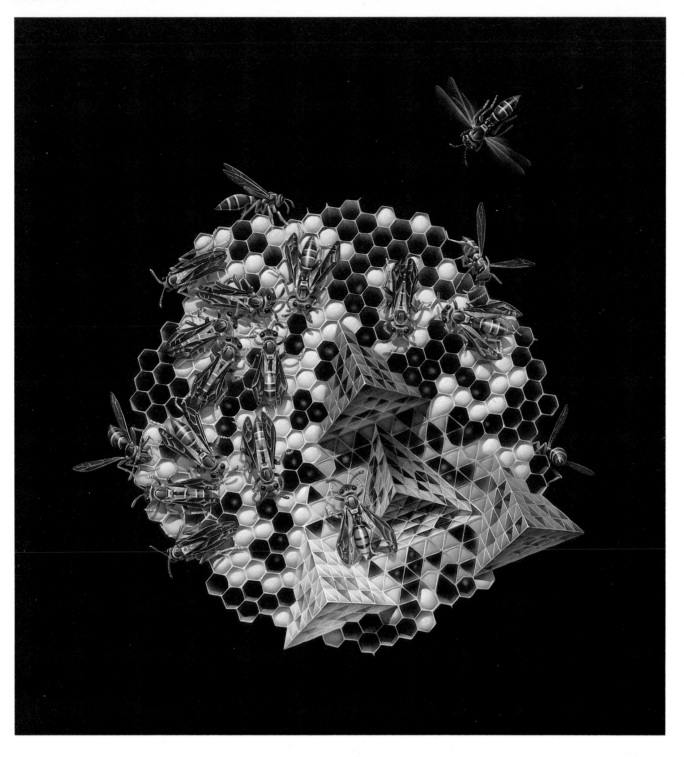

ILLUSTRATOR
THOM ANG

MEDIUM
MIXED MEDIA

ART DIRECTOR
ALLEN SPIEGEL

CLIENT
ALLEN SPIEGEL
FINE ARTS

● 318

ILLUSTRATOR
EZRA TUCKER

MEDIUM
ACRYLIC
ON CANVAS

● 319

SELF-PROMOTIONAL/
UNPUBLISHED

ILLUSTRATOR
THOMAS L. FLUHARTY

MEDIUM
PASTEL

● 320

MEDICAL

HONORABLE MENTION

KEITH KASNOT

HONORABLE MENTION

KEITH KASNOT

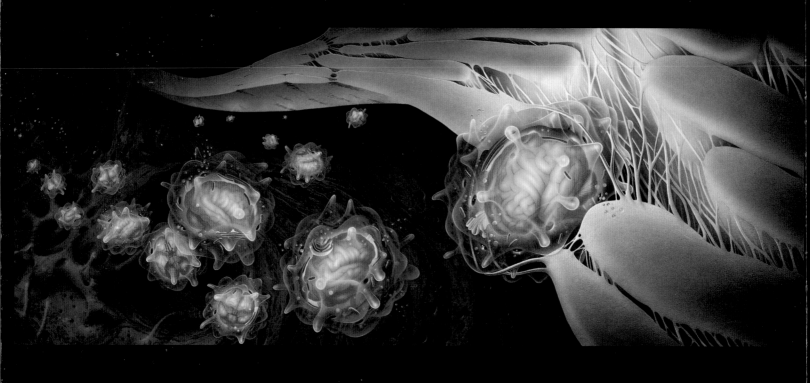

[MEDICAL HONORABLE MENTION]

ILLUSTRATOR
KEITH KASNOT

MEDIUM
TRANSPARENT PIGMENT DYES ON HAND MARBLED PAPER

ART DIRECTOR
MIKE DONALDSON

CLIENT
W. L. GORE AND ASSOCIATES

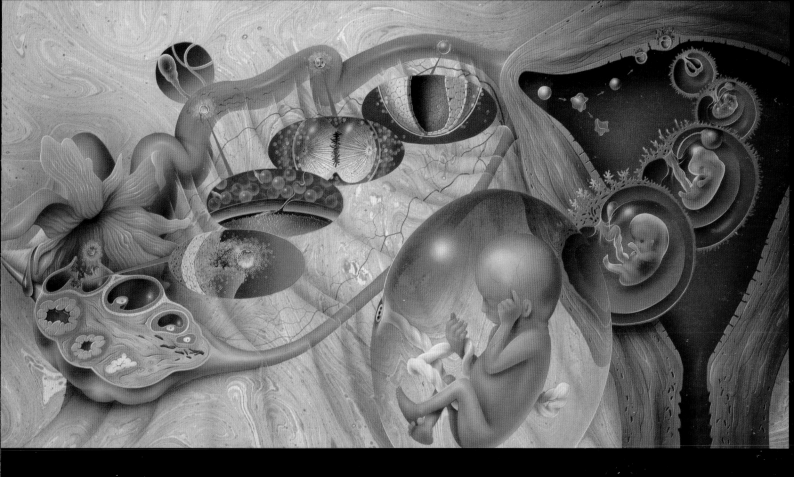

STUDENT

GOLD MEDAL

E. TAGE LARSEN

SILVER MEDAL

KITTY MEEK

BRONZE MEDAL

KITTY MEEK

[STUDENT GOLD MEDAL]

ILLUSTRATOR
JENNIFER ANDO

MEDIUM
ACRYLIC

INSTRUCTOR
DAVID MOCARSKI,
ART CENTER

● 326

ILLUSTRATOR
JENNIFER
JARMEL

MEDIUM
OIL

●○ 327

ILLUSTRATOR
JUI ISHIDA

MEDIUM
ACRYLIC &
PRISMACOLOR

INSTRUCTOR
JIM SALVATI,
ART CENTER

○● 328

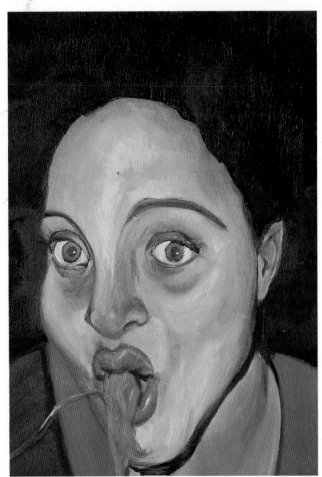

STUDENT

ILLUSTRATOR
SEAN COONS

INSTRUCTOR
RICHARD DOWNS,
ART CENTER

●○ 329

ILLUSTRATOR
ADAM ELESH

MEDIUM
MULTI MEDIA

INSTRUCTOR
DAVID MOCARSKI,
ART CENTER

○● 330

ILLUSTRATOR
JUI ISHIDA

MEDIUM
ACRYLIC &
PRISMACOLOR

INSTRUCTOR
JIM SALVATI,
ART CENTER

● 331

MARK H. ADAMS
1766 E. 3rd Street
Long Beach, CA 90802
310-435-0344
278

RICHARD ADKINS
6406 Bryn Mawr Drive
Hollywood, CA 90068
213-463-1018 fax:213-463-4340
264

MICHAEL ALBRECHTSEN
8816 W. 95th Terrace
Overland Park, KS 66212
913-642-5228
131

PAUL ALEXANDER
37 Pine Mountain Rd.
West Redding, CT 06896
203-544-9293
254

JENNIFER ANDO
23542 Evalyn Avenue
Torrance, CA 90505
310-378-7914
326

RICHARD ANDRI
165 Park Row #15 B
New York, NY 10038
212-962-9423
165

THOM ANG
1622 ½ Bank St.
South Pasadena, CA 91030
818-441-0424
195, 318

SCOTT ANGLE
21051 Barbados Circle
Huntington Beach, CA 92646
714-960-8485
30

DON ARDAY
616 Arbor Creek Drive
Desoto, TX 75115
214-223-6235 fax: 214-223-6280
114, 309

DON ASMUSSEN
3975 Hortensia St. #6-E
San Diego, CA 92110
619-298-0414
93, 109, 146, 162, 221

SERGIO BARADAT
210 W 70th St. #1606
New York, NY 10023
212-721-2588 fax: 212-982-9363
3, 202

BRYN BARNARD
914 Rock Moss Ave.
Newark, DE 19711
302-456-3909
152, 244

GARY BASEMAN
443 12th Street #20
Brooklyn, NY 11215
718-499-9358
159

CHERIE BENDER
12105 NE 6th Ave. #404
North Miami, FL 33161
305-891-1629
227

MIKE BENNY
2773 Knollwood
Cameron Park, CA 95682
916-677-9142
Award for Excellence, 4, 248

MARK BISCHEL
4419 Roanoke Pkwy #3-South
Kansas City, MO 64110
816-753-4852
196

PHIL BOATWRIGHT
2342 Stillwater Dr.
Mesquite, TX 75181
214-222-7571 fax: 214-222-2398
16, 50, 128, 129, 144, 149

MARTHA ANNE BOOTH
990 Acacia St., PO Box 208
Montara, CA 94037
415-728-8332
246, 269

DAVID BOWERS
100 Scott Way
Carnegie, PA 15106
412-276-7224
243, 288

DOUG BOWLES
7 West 70th Terrace
Kansas City, MO 64113
816-523-6324
98, 207, 270, 290

BRALDT BRALDS
183 Lower San Pedro
Espanola, NM 87532
505-747-1716 fax: 505-753-1977
Best of Show, 53, 62, 65, 69, 81,102

CALEF BROWN
1400 Concordia Ave.
Austin, TX 78722
512-478-5389
100

MARC BURCKHARDT
1101 Shoal Creek Blvd. #10
Austin, TX 78701
512-474-9781
191, 193

ROBERT BURGER
145 Kingwood Stockton Road
Stockton, NJ 08559
609-397-3737 fax: 609-397-3666
280, 302

THOM BUTTNER
1400 South Highway Drive
Fenton, MO 63099
314-827-2955 fax: 314-827-6035
27

KEVIN CARMONA
2058 Sixth St.
La Verne, CA 91750
909-593-5439
279

ALAN CARR
51 Dean St. Apt. 2
Brooklyn, NY 11201
718-596-8850
222

VIDAL CENTENO
1734 Madison Ave. #10-E
New York, NY 10029
718-365-9749
277

JOE CEPEDA
3370 Ivar Avenue
Rosemead, CA 91770
818-288-8205
115

LINA CHESAK
2265 Idylwood Station Lane
Falls Church, VA 22043
703-573-4230
56, 158

JAEEUN CHOI
70 Clark St. #6 D
Brooklyn, NY 11201
718-237-0216
275

ROB CLAYTON
10730 E. Bethany Dr. #204
Aurora, CO 80014
303-337-5952
122

TED COCONIS
PO Box 758
Cedar Key, FL 32625
904-543-5720
287

DICK COLE
21925 Hyde Road
Sonoma, CA 95476
707-939-8853 fax: 707-935-9075
169

PETER COLE
5920 Oak
Kansas City, MO 64113
816-471-2327
299

BOB COMMANDER
1565 W. Village Round Drive
Park City, UT 84060
801-649-4356
293

BYRON COONS
2282 Amherst St.
Palo Alto, CA 94306
415-856-0102
306

SEAN COONS
3127 Foothill Blvd. #102
La Crescenta, CA 91214
818-248-3923
329

TREVOR COPENHAVER
3065 3rd Ave. #4
San Diego, CA 92103
619-299-6709
282

ROBERT CRAWFORD
123 Minortown Rd.
Woodbury, CT 06798
203-266-0059
157

MIKE CRESSY
3605 SW 112th St.
Seattle, WA 98146
206-243-7338
150

DAVE CUTLER
7 Sunrise Ridge
Florida, NY 10921
914-651-1580 fax: 914-651-1590
125

JAMES DIETZ
2203 13th Ave. East
Seattle, WA 78102
206-325-2857
25, 26

C. MICHAEL DUDASH
RR #1 Box 2803
Moretown, VT 05660
802-496-6400
14, 34, 249

JOHN DYKES
17 Morningside Dr. South
Westport, CT 06880
203-222-8150 fax: 203-222-8155
139, 154

CAMERON EAGLE
1911 NW 29th
Oklahoma City, OK 73096
405-525-6676
36, 314

SAHAK EKSHIAN
23875 Ventura Blvd. #104
Calabasas, CA 91302
818-223-8400 fax: 818-223-8404
228

ADAM ELESH
1475 Oakdale Dr.
Pasadena, CA 91106
818-568-0936
330

JAMES ENDICOTT
3509 N. College
Newburg, OR 97132
503-538-5466 fax: 503-538-5792
96

JOHN ENGLISH
5844 Fontana Dr.
Fairway, KS 66205
913-831-4830 fax: 913-831-4916
1, 23, 46, 49, 259

KERNE ERICKSON
26571 Oliva, PO Box 2175
Mission Viejo, CA 92690
714-364-1141 fax: 800-835-1949
44, 45

THOMAS L. FLUHARTY
200 Rector Place, 41F
New York, NY 10280
212-986-4746 fax: 212-786-4350
176, 263, 320

BRIAN FOX
29 Massasoit Street
Somerset, MA 02725
508-674-0511
234

DOUGLAS FRASER
1742 10th Avenue SW
Calgary, Alberta. Canada T3C-0J8
403-244-6636
75

LISA FRENCH
355 Molino Avenue
Long Beach, CA 90814
310-434-5277
272, 295

SARAJO FRIEDEN
1910 N. Serrano Ave.
Los Angeles, CA 90027
213-462-5045 fax: 213-462-5083
315

DIANA FRITCH
28315 Driza
Mission Viejo, CA 92692
714-458-2356
292

WAYNE GALLIPOLI
14 Gilbert Street D-3
West Haven, CT 06516
203-937-8384
273

TOM GARRETT
623 3rd Ave SE
Minneapolis, MN 55414
612-331-3123
91, 200

JEFF GEORGE
11716 ½ E. 215th St.
Lakewood, CA 90715
310-924-0123
212, 218

DEANNA GLAD
PO Box 1962
San Pedro, CA 90733
310-831-6274
19

RANDY GLASS
1950 Wattles Dr.
Los Angeles, CA 90046
213-851-6555
220

ELISSÉ JO GOLDSTEIN
182 E 95th St. 2-K
New York, NY 10128
212-534-3594
285

DANILO GONZALEZ
324 N. Marengo Ave.
Alhambra, CA 91801
818-300-0132
66

CARTER GOODRICH
100 Angell St #1
Providence, RI 02906
800-992-4552
99, 170, 179

DAN GOOZEE
22534 Maldon St.
West Hills, CA 91304
818-887-5624
231, 260

JULIA GRAN
3240 Henry Hudson Pkwy #6H
Bronx, NY 10463
718-601-8820 fax: 718-601-8266
301

COURTNEY GRANNER
328 N. Fifth St.
Patterson, CA 95363
209-892-2973
103, 108, 143, 156

PAULINE GREENE
70 Village Parkway
Santa Monica, CA 90405
310-450-4200 fax: 310-450-3936
296

DAVID GROVE
382 Union Street
San Francisco, CA 94133
415-433-2100
145

DAVID HALEY
1400 South Highway Drive
Fenton, MO 63099
314-827-2955 fax: 314-827-6035
262

VIRGINIA HALSTEAD
4336 Gayle Drive
Tarzana, CA 91356
818-705-4353
206

PAM-ELA HARRELSON
2707 Beechmont Drive
Dallas, TX 75228
214-321-6061 fax: 214-321-7424
30, 39

BRYAN HAYNES
PO Box 111, #2 Fairfield
St. Albans, MO 63073
314-451-5115 fax: 314-742-5606
55, 71

PETER HEER
500 Molino St. #306
Los Angeles, CA 90013
213-617-1282
297

HAYES HENDERSON
815 Burke St.
Winston-Salem, NC 27101
910-748-1364
116

MIKE HODGES
734 Indian Beach Circle
Sarasota, FL 34234
813-351-2226
216

EUGENE HOFFMAN
1811 12th Street
Greeley, CO 80631
303-351-7991
181, 258, 311

SPONSORS

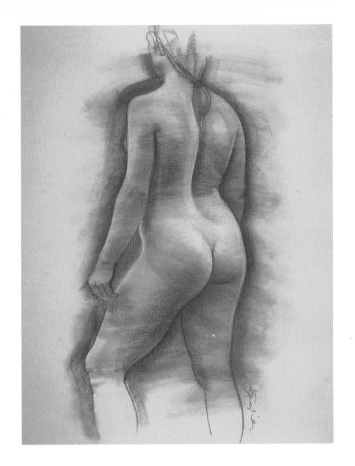

FIRST SESSION
May 14 - June 16

SECOND SESSION
July 2 - August 4

MARK ENGLISH
JOHN COLLIER
ERIC DINYER
JOHN ENGLISH
BART FORBES
GARY KELLEY
SKIP LIEPKE
C.F. PAYNE
JACK UNRUH

THE ILLUSTRATION ACADEMY

THE ILLUSTRATION ACADEMY offers art students and professionals the opportunity to study with some of the most successful and exciting illustrators working today. See the art and talk to the artists who set the pace in the field. Improve your work, your work habits, and your portfolios.

THE ILLUSTRATION ACADEMY offers one two-week, and two five-week intensive workshops to be held in the summer of 1995 at William Jewell College in Liberty, Missouri. Room and board are available.

FOR MORE INFORMATION WRITE TO:
The Illustration Academy
512 Lakeside Court
Liberty, MO 64068

OR CALL:
816.781-7304

DESIGN MATHEMATICS

SOLUTIONS

At the Warren Group, successful
design solves problems. It all
adds up. Teamwork + creativity +
experience. Here the whole really
is greater than the sum of its
parts. Because we work to balance
the best possible equation of
copy, art and design.

In ten years, we've won many
prestigious awards. But even more
important, we've helped clients
achieve their goals, often
within difficult time and cost
constraints. All while keeping
ourselves intimate and responsive.
Take a look at a few of our
positive solutions. Then call.
Or come by for pi.

THE WARREN GROUP

622 Hampton Drive
Venice USA
310.396.6316

Thanks Squared: Candace Pearson, Copy   Julie Scott, Illustration   Craig Mohr, Photography   JT&A, Film Separations

SOCIETY OF ILLUSTRATORS OF LOS ANGELES
MEMBERSHIP AND ILLUSTRATION WEST INFORMATION

Nationwide in scope, The Society of Illustrators of Los Angeles is a non-profit organization of professional and student illustrators dedicated to education and social interaction among illustrators and the community at large. There are monthly educational seminars and workshops open to the public, where issues of importance are presented to illustrators and people working in the graphics arts field. Illustration West, now in its 34th consecutive year, is the largest juried exhibition of illustration work west of New York, with over 300 original works exhibited. SILA has a student scholarship program, along with other community service projects such as an Air Force Art program, Sheriff's Documentary Art program, and The Children's Hospital program. Membership is open to all professional illustrators, full-time illustration students, or those allied to the field.

Please write to the address below for further information on membership in our organization, to order additional copies of this annual, or an entry form for Illustration West 34.

THE SOCIETY OF ILLUSTRATORS OF LOS ANGELES
116 The Plaza Pasadena
Pasadena, CA. 91101
818-952-SILA

Illustration by Robert Rodriguez